Series Editor

PAOLO BERTINETTI

Professor of English Literature,
University of Padua

Oscar Wilde
Short Stories

Introduction, notes and activities by
BRIAN HODGKISS
Turin Polytechnic

CIDEB

Illustrations by Anne Hodgkiss

First edition: December 1994

10 9 8 7 6 5 4 3 2 1

ISBN 88-7754-153 9

Printed in Italy by Istituto Grafico Bertello, Borgo San Dalmazzo (CN)

Contents

Phonetic Symbols

Vowels

[ɪ]	*as in*	s**i**x
[i]	"	happ**y**
[iː]	"	s**ee**
[e]	"	r**e**d
[æ]	"	h**a**t
[ɑː]	"	c**ar**
[ɒ]	"	d**o**g
[ɔː]	"	d**oor**
[ʊ]	"	p**u**t
[uː]	"	f**oo**d
[ʌ]	"	c**u**p
[ə]	"	**a**bout
[ɜː]	"	g**ir**l

Diphthongs

[eɪ]	*as in*	m**a**de
[aɪ]	"	f**i**ve
[aʊ]	"	h**ou**se
[ɔɪ]	"	b**oy**
[əʊ]	"	h**o**me
[ɪə]	"	b**eer**
[eə]	"	h**air**
[ʊə]	"	p**oor**

Consonants

[b]	*as in*	**b**ed
[k]	"	**c**at
[tʃ]	"	**church**
[d]	"	**d**ay
[f]	"	**f**oot
[g]	"	**g**ood
[dʒ]	"	pa**ge**
[h]	"	**h**ow
[j]	"	**y**es
[l]	"	**l**eg
[m]	"	**mum**
[n]	"	**nine**
[ŋ]	"	si**ng**
[p]	"	**p**en
[r]	"	**r**ed
[s]	"	**s**oon
[z]	"	**z**oo
[ʃ]	"	**sh**ow
[ʒ]	"	mea**s**ure
[t]	"	**t**ea
[θ]	"	**th**in
[ð]	"	**th**is
[v]	"	**v**oice
[w]	"	**w**ine

[ˈ] represents primary stress in the syllable which follows

[ˌ] represents secondary stress in the syllable which follows

[r] indicates that the final "r" is only pronounced before a word beginning with a vowel sound (British English). In American English, the "r" is usually pronounced before both consonants and vowel sounds.

Wilde lampooned in a pamphlet.

Introduction

Wilde's Life

Oscar Fingal O'Flahertie Wills Wilde, born in Dublin on 16 October 1854, was the second son of Sir William Wilde and Jane Elgee. Sir William was an eminent eye specialist while Lady Wilde was an Irish nationalist poet, who wrote under the name of Speranza. Both were students of Irish legend, folklore and history, so that Wilde grew up in an atmosphere that influenced his imaginative growth. Story and fable were part of his inheritance.

Wilde was educated at Portora Royal School in Enniskillen and Trinity College, Dublin, where, under the influence of the classical scholar, John Pentland Mahaffy, he studied Latin and Greek literature, which further stimulated his imagination. In 1874 he won the Berkeley Gold Medal for Greek and, in 1875, a scholarship to Magdalen College Oxford, where he became famous for his wit, his ostentatious dress and his eccentric behaviour as well as for his aestheticism. At Oxford he was influenced by John Ruskin, who emphasized the moral dimension of art, and Walter Pater, for whom, in his devotion to aestheticism, the pursuit of beauty was the chief purpose of life. Wilde later tended to dismiss the moral element in art, embracing the doctrine of aestheticism and insisting that art was valuable only for its aesthetic qualities; however, in practice morality, even if unconventional, was never absent from his work, not even in such an apparently trivial comedy as *The Importance of Being Earnest*. There is quite clearly a moral dimension to each of the stories in this volume, never more so than in "The Birthday of the Infanta", where Wilde's aestheticism is most evident.

Wilde finished his studies at Oxford in 1878 with two great successes, when he won the Newdigate Prize for his poem "Ravenna" and was then awarded a double first class honours, a rare achievement. From Oxford he moved to

London where he soon became a social success because of his wit and his brilliant conversational powers. During this period he cultivated the friendship of a number of actresses, including Lily Langtree (who was to become mistress of the Prince of Wales), Ellen Terry and Sarah Bernhardt. He was to be seen on all the right social occasions – first nights, parties and private views – sometimes wearing "aesthetic dress", for which he was often mocked, and establishing himself as a kind of priest of aestheticism, which he compared to the Italian Renaissance and Romanticism as "a sort of new birth of the spirit of man". In 1881 he published his first volume of poetry to a mixed critical reception and completed a lecture tour of the United States in 1882 (he was to visit America again for the unfavourably received first performance of his play *Vera* in New York in 1883). Wilde's experiences in the United States clearly influenced his amusing, somewhat satirical portrayal of the Otis family in "The Canterville Ghost". Here is Richard Ellmann's description of his arrival in America:

> The *Arizona* docked in New York harbor on the evening of 2 January 1882. It was too late to clear quarantine until the following morning. The press, avid to see Wilde, could not wait. Enterprising reporters "came out of the sea", as Wilde picturesquely noticed, their pens still wet with brine. Wilde was in the captain's cabin and emerged to greet them in the great green coat that hung down almost to his feet. It was subjected to close inspection: the collar and cuffs were trimmed with seal or otter, and so was the material for the round cap, variously described as a smoking cap or turban. Beneath the coat could be discerned a shirt with a wide Lord Byron collar, and a sky-blue necktie, vaguely reminiscent of the costume of a modern mariner. He wore patent leather shoes on his small feet. [1]

Despite the eccentric clothes, however, the press, who had been led to expect an effeminate figure, were surprised to find instead this tall broad-shouldered man with a voice that was anything but feminine. This did not prevent journalists from subjecting Wilde to a barrage of questions and from reporting, usually in distorted form, every word he said. One of the most famous remarks attributed to him (and it is possible that he actually said it) was when, in response to the customs officer's question, "Have you anything to declare?", he was reported to have said, "I have nothing to declare except my genius". Although the tour was initially a great social success, he later encountered many problems. In Boston, for example, he was to speak in the Music Hall. Despite the snow that had fallen, the house was full – except for the first two rows, which remained strangely empty until just before the speaker was due to appear. At that moment sixty Harvard students, dressed in the extravagant manner associated with aestheticism and particularly with Wilde, took their places in the empty seats. They were all wearing kneebreeches, for which Wilde had been mocked, and each wore a fair wig and carried in his hand a sunflower, which, together with the lily, was a symbol of aestheticism. Their leader "lounged, limp and listless and vacant eyed, to a seat",[2] in an attempt to ridicule Wilde's mannerisms. Wilde, however, was master of the situation and created a great deal of laughter at the expense of those who had come to mock him. Forewarned of the students' intentions, instead of wearing the ostentatious clothes his American audiences had come to expect, he "had donned conventional dinner jacket and trousers, and hinted at iconoclasm only in the unusually wide cravat which reached nearly to his shoulders on either side".[3] He began his lecture with a compliment to Boston, "the only city in America which has influenced thought in Europe," then, apparently casually and with a smile, turned his attention to the Harvard students. "I see about me certain signs of an aesthetic movement," he began. "I see certain young men, who are no doubt sincere, but I can assure them that they are no more than caricatures". These remarks were received with laughter and his epigram that "caricature is the tribute mediocrity pays to genius" was loudly applauded.[4] He continued, "As I look around me, I am impelled for the first time to breath a fervent prayer, 'Save me from my disciples,'" which, according to Pearson, "brought the house down". He went on to assure the students before him that there was "more to the movement of aestheticism than kneebreeches and sunflowers". Other of Wilde's experiences in North America included a visit to Niagara Falls, with which he at first professed to be disappointed (they were, he suggested with his customary wit, 'the first disappointment in the married life of many Americans who spend their honeymoon there') and another to the Rocky Mountains, where he met and had dinner with a group of miners at the bottom of a mine. Commenting on the dinner, he reported:

> 'The first course was whiskey, the second whiskey, the third whiskey, all the courses were whiskey, but still they called it supper'. In the evening he went to the Casino where he found 'the miners and the female friends of the miners, and in one corner a pianist – sitting at a piano over which there was this notice: "Please don't shoot the pianist; he is doing his best."' Reflecting on his experiences of the United States with that combination of seriousness and absurdity for which he is famous he commented: 'The crude commercialism of America, its materializing spirit, its indifference to the poetical side of things, and its lack of imagination and of high unobtainable ideals, are entirely due to that country having adopted for its national hero a man who, according to his own confession, was incapable of telling a lie; and it is not too much to say that the story of George Washington and of the cherry-tree has done more harm, and in a shorter space of time, than any other moral tale in the whole of literature ... and the amusing part of the whole thing is that the story of the cherry-tree is an absolute myth.'

According to Pearson, Wilde never spoke in favour of America or its inhabitants, because he believed that for the American "Art has no marvel, and Beauty no meaning, and the Past no message."[5]

In 1883 he went on another lecture tour, this time of the United Kingdom. One of his lectures on this tour was entitled "The House Beautiful", indicating his concern with

Sketches of Oscar Wilde in America.

the aesthetics of interior design, and another, "The Value of Art in Modern Life", is a statement of aesthetic principles. We can see Wilde's love of visual beauty in all the stories here, and his interest in interior design is most clearly shown in "The Birthday of the Infanta", with its rich and detailed descriptions of the different chambers of the royal palace that the dwarf passes through.

On 29 May, 1884 Wilde married Constance Lloyd, whom he described as "a grave, slight, violet-eyed little Artemis, with great coils of heavy brown hair which make her flower-like head droop like a blossom". The relationship with Constance, because of Wilde's homosexuality, was to become a tragic one.

When the Wildes moved to Tite Street, Chelsea, Edwin Godwin set out to decorate the house in a style which he and Wilde intended to establish new standards in interior design. This concern with design can be seen in the visual descriptions found in a number of the stories in this book (particularly in "The Birthday of the Infanta"), where we find reflected Wilde's interest not only in interior design but in costume, painting and architecture.

Constance Wilde gave birth to two sons, Cyril, in June 1885, and Vyvyan, in November 1886. Wilde published "The Canterville Ghost" in 1887 and in 1888, *The Happy Prince and Other Tales,* which established his reputation as a writer, being well received by, among others, Walter Pater, who wrote to Wilde: "I'm confined to my room with gout, but have been consoling myself with The Happy Prince, and feel it would be ungrateful not to send a line to tell you how delightful I have found him and his companions. I hardly know whether to admire more the wise wit of "The Remarkable Rocket" or the beauty and tenderness of "The Selfish Giant": the latter is certainly perfect in its kind."[6] Pater paid Wilde a further compliment, telling him that the whole book was written in "pure English". The *Athenaeum* praised the stories for their "charming fancies and quaint humour" and compared Wilde to Hans Christian Andersen.[7] During the following years he published further stories and a number of important essays, including "The Decay of Lying", which asserted that "art never expresses anything but itself" and that, far from being a creation of its time, art is usually "in direct opposition" to its own time, frequently looking forward to the future and never merely reproducing its age. Nor does Art imitate Life and Nature; rather it is the other way round: "Life imitates Art more than Art imitates Life". These are challenging views, but, as we have seen, in practice Wilde does express morality in his work, as in the stories printed here. In 1890, Wilde published his only novel *The Picture of Dorian Gray,* which was reissued in revised form in 1891. This novel, as Ellmann points out,[8] shows the dangers of aestheticism, since Wilde could no longer be said to advocate, in any simple way, the doctrine of art for art's sake, something which we can also deduce from these stories.

Having written *Vera* and *The Duchess of Padua* in the early 1890s, Wilde turned again to the drama in the early 1890s, writing *Salomé* (1891-2), *Lady Windermere's Fan* (performed February, 1892), *A Woman of No Importance* (performed April, 1893), *An Ideal Husband* (first performance, 3 January, 1895) and his masterpiece, *The Importance of Being Earnest* (first performance, 14 February, 1895). During this period of intense artistic activity Wilde became romantically involved with Lord Alfred Douglas, and it was this affair which was to lead to his tragic downfall when he was at the height of his fame and artistic success. Lord Alfred's father, the Marquess of Queensbury, enraged by Wilde's relationship with his son, accused him, in the street and in writing on a visiting card, of being a homosexual. Since homosexuality was a criminal offence at that time, Wilde sued Queensbury for libel but lost his case, only to find himself arrested and tried for the crime Queensbury had accused him of. Found guilty after two trials, Wilde was imprisoned for two years. While in prison, he wrote a long letter to Lord Alfred Douglas, *De Profundis*, in which he claimed to have found the consolation of Christ, and *The Ballad of Reading Gaol*, in which he wrote about the isolation and brutality of prison life, about the cruelty of murder, and about the cruelty of the society that inflicts punishment for such crimes. After his release from prison in May, 1897, Wilde lived mainly in France, but spent periods in Switzerland and Italy. He never succeeded in regaining his inspiration and died in Paris on 30 November, 1900.

The Stories in this Volume

When Wilde chose to write in the form of the fairy tale he was using a form that was popular, and, as Isobel Murray points out, gave scope for invention. Murray continues: "Wilde's mother and Yeats had both published collections of Irish folk-tales, and Andrew Lang ... began his series of multicoloured "fairy books" in 1899. Hans Andersen had established the fairy-tale, and there is no doubt that Wilde saturated himself in Andersen before producing *The Happy Prince* – and also *A House of Pomegranates* ... It would be tedious to detail the resemblances [but] themes that recur in Andersen certainly occur in Wilde ... and Wilde probably learned from Andersen the witty, deflating touches which graced the stories, but never, even in "The Selfish Giant", is he betrayed into such depths of sentimentality as Anderson. He takes over witty talking animals and objects..., but he avoids Andersen's cloying moments, and generally transcends him. Andersen wrote far, far more fairy-tales than Wilde; he did not write more that survive".[9] Of the stories in *The Happy Prince* (four of which are included here) Wilde wrote: they are "meant partly for children and partly for those who have kept the childlike faculties of wonder and joy". This can also be applied to the other stories, "The Canterville Ghost" and "The Birthday of the Infanta", which, behind their apparent simplicity, contain what Wilde called a "subtle strangeness". Through all the stories Wilde can be felt as a welcome presence, commenting wittily on character and behaviour, always gentle, always kindly, always exposing cruelty. This presence of the author is what, above all, gives the stories their flavour. His intense interest in colours, forms, textures, paintings and architecture pervades almost all the stories, giving the prose style a richness which some might consider excessive.

Despite the constant presence of the author, each story has its distinctive qualities and the narrative method and atmosphere differ from story to story. "The Canterville Ghost" was written after Wilde's American lecture tour of 1882 and its satire of American people and ideas must have been at least in part derived from his experiences on that tour, which were not entirely happy, since, as we have seen, he suffered considerable mockery, particularly at the hands of American journalists. Wilde, however, was not a vengeful man and his satire seems gentle, not in the least vicious. In any case, English customs and traditions receive an equal share of gentle mockery in the story, giving it a delightful balance between the way in which both English and American attitudes are ridiculed, not harshly, but as amusing examples of the folly of human behaviour. In this story, Wilde takes the conventions of the ghost story and constructs out of them a delightful comedy, though even the comedy is distinctive in the way it moves to its tender sad-sweet end, where the poor ghost is redeemed by the capacity for love of a young girl, Virginia, who, because of the pity aroused in her by the sufferings of the ghost, is able to shed tears for him, thus, according to an old prophecy, releasing him from his torments. In this story the practicality of the Otis family can be seen as a characteristic opposed to the imagination; only Virginia possesses a romantic, imaginative sensibility in contrast to the blunt common sense of the males of the family. Talking about the difference between American men and women Wilde suggested that American girls were 'pretty and charming – little oases of pretty unreasonableness in a vast desert of practical common sense'. Of American men he said 'I can stand brute force, but brute reason is quite unbearable,' and summed up: 'American women are charming, but American men – alas!' Even so, one can hardly describe the Otis males as villains: Mr Otis, for example, is an honourable man, even if entirely lacking in imagination, and the twins are naughty rather than vicious. One point about this ghost story is that there are no villains, though the ghost had behaved villainously in the past. Faced by the "brute reason" and the "desert of common sense" of the Otis males the once terrifying ghost dwindles into a figure evoking pity rather than terror.

Another object of Wilde's mockery in the story is the American love of patent medicines and compounds such as "Pinkerton's Champion Remover and Paragon Detergent", while the ironic reference to "the importance of Boston in the development of the world soul" reflects the opinion Wilde formed of that city during his stay there. To counterbalance the criticism of American attitudes, we have frequent mocking references to the English aristocracy (an object of satire in other works by Wilde as, for example, in the figure of Lady Bracknell in *The Importance of Being Earnest*). Further, as Isobel Murray points out, "there is constant mockery of English stage melodrama in the various 'parts' played by the Ghost, and mockery of aristocratic family pride in the tales of death by fright passed down from one generation to another. The readiness of the English to believe in ghosts, even to the point of expiry, is mocked as surely as the American commonsensical refusal to believe."[10]

Each of the four stories from *The Happy Prince* also has a distinctive quality, though all of them, even "The Remarkable Rocket" (the one comic story in that volume), share that peculiar Wildean gentleness and sensitivity. Wilde used to read these stories to his two sons at bedtime from his large paper copy of the edition.

The title story of the volume is, apart from anything else, the work of Wilde the socialist. The tears of the Happy Prince are shed on account of the cruelty and injustice he was once, in his privileged position, blind to. Losing his physical beauty, he achieves a new spiritual beauty and tenderness of heart that he had never possessed in life. Wilde himself wrote that these stories were "an attempt to mirror modern life in a form remote from reality – to deal with modern problems in a mode that is ideal and not imitative". Taking this hint, we can see the city of "The Happy Prince" as a reflection of large English cities, especially London, in the Victorian age; cities in which squalor, crime and poverty existed side by side with riches. The story is also about friendship, kindness of heart, selflessness, the capacity to love and make sacrifices for others, as well as mockery of self-importance in the town councillors. In this tale, Wilde uses the traditional magic number of three, found in so many myths and legends, as a means of structuring his narrative, mirroring modern life, to use his words, through the form of a fairy-tale. There seems to be also at least one personal reference in the story. Once, on being asked how he had happened to fall in love with his wife, Constance, Wilde replied, 'She scarcely ever speaks. I am always wondering what her thoughts are like,' and in the story the swallow falls out of love with a reed, partly because "She has no conversation." [11]

The theme of "The Nightingale and the Rose" may have been suggested by the love of the nightingale for the rose in Persian mythology and its most likely English source is the Irish poet Thomas Moore's "Lalla Rookh" (1817). The theme can also be found in Byron's *Don Juan*, vi, 87 (1824) and elsewhere in English literature. As in "The Happy Prince", an important theme is self-sacrifice, the desire to help another even if it costs one's own self-destruction. Wilde wrote to a friend, Thomas Hutchinson:

> I am afraid that I don't think as much of the young Student as you do. He seems to me a rather shallow young man... The nightingale is the true lover if there is one. She, at least, is Romance – and the Student and the Girl are, like most of us, unworthy of Romance. So, at least, it seems to me, but I like to fancy there are many meanings in the Tale – for in writing it ... I did not start with the idea and clothe it in form, but began with a form and strove to make it beautiful enough to have many secrets and many answers.

The sadness of the story derives from the apparent pointlessness of the nightingale's sacrifice since the story ends ironically with the girl's showing no appreciation of the rose, the symbol of love, and with the student's going back to his arid books, apparently incapable of feeling any true depth of emotion.

Some may argue that in these two stories Wilde fails to avoid sentimentality, while others would say that the author's sense of irony saves the stories from that charge. It is "The Selfish Giant", however, that many feel comes closest to sentimentality, particularly in the attempt to equate the child with Christ. Like Christ, the child suffers from wounds and promises to take the Giant to Paradise, thus bringing about his redemption through love. The child makes this explicit when he says: "these are the wounds of Love." Wilde's motives are not in doubt: he wants to assert the value of love and self-sacrifice for another, but his symbolism may be felt to be too obvious. One must remember, however, differences between our taste and that of the Victorians: to us, Victorian literature often crosses the border between feeling and sentimentality, with Dickens as perhaps the most obvious example among great writers. Wilde is also drawing heavily on the Christian tradition of the child as symbol of grace, as, for example, in St Matthew, ch. 18, v. 3: "Except ye be converted, and become as little children, ye shall not enter into the kingdom of heaven", or St Matthew, ch. 18, v. 5: "Whoso shall receive one such little child in my name receiveth me. / But whoso shall offend one of these little ones which believe in me, it were better for him that a millstone were hanged about his neck, and that he were drowned in the depth of the sea." Whatever one's conclusion about the charge of sentimentality, the story should be seen in both a Victorian and Biblical tradition.

"The Remarkable Rocket", which makes use of the convention of talking objects and animals, may be more acceptable to modern taste. It is an amusing study of vanity and the loss of a sense of reality deriving from that vice. The rocket, in believing in "the immense inferiority of everybody else" to himself, is guilty of one of the traditional seven deadly sins, pride. Even so, his fall may be seen as having a certain pathos. Critics like Isobel Murray and H. Montgomery Hyde[12] have also pointed out how the rocket foreshadows "the aging, narcissistic dandies of the novel and the plays, who will also try to manipulate the world to their advantage".[13] This story, above all the others selected here, suggests the presence of Wilde, the future successful comic dramatist. Much of the story, in fact, advances mainly by means of dialogue.

"The Birthday of the Infanta" is perhaps the most difficult story here, not because of its ideas but because of the exceptionally wide vocabulary used. The story originally appeared in 1889 and was republished in the collection, *A House of Pomegranates* (1891). Wilde said he considered it his best story and dedicated it to his wife, Constance. Important themes in this story are those of suffering for love, the association of beauty and cruelty, and the rejection by society of those who are "different". This last theme occurs frequently in much of Wilde's work and probably reflects his own feeling that he, as a homosexual, was an "outsider", despite his apparent popularity in high society during that period of his life (his tragic rejection by that society would not take place until a few years after the publication of this story). The theme of the association of beauty and cruelty appears again in *The Picture of Dorian Gray* and receives its fullest treatment in *Salomé,* first published in French in 1893 and in England (in Lord Alfred Douglas's translation) in 1894. Wilde criticises the cruelty of the Spanish court in general and of the hard-heartedness of the Infanta, who can see nothing in the Dwarf except a cause for sadistic laughter. We have an opposition in this story between beauty combined with heartlessness, on the one hand, and ugliness combined with tender feeling on the other.

In *A House of Pomegranates* and in "The Birthday of the Infanta", in particular, we have a great deal more visual description than in *The Happy Prince* volume. Wilde called "The Birthday of the Infanta" "a study in black and silver". Another way of describing the story might be that it presents a contrast between nature (represented by the Dwarf and

Wilde's second book of fairy-tales, 1891.

his forest home) and art and artifice (represented by the royal court and palace). The rich descriptions of the court, its rituals, its chambers, its tapestries, its costumes are evidence of Wilde's passionate interest in costume, décor and art.

A number of themes recur in the stories: redemption through love ("The Canterville Ghost", "The Happy Prince", "The Nightingale and the Rose", "The Selfish Giant"); self-sacrifice (the last three stories of those just mentioned); self-delusion (the student in "The Nightingale and the Rose", "The Remarkable Rocket", and, in a different, more touching way, the Dwarf in "The Birthday of the Infanta"); illusion and reality (a theme present in all the stories in one way or another). Other themes, like the association of beauty with cruelty, materialism versus imagination, the Outsider, and the contrast between beauty and ugliness were life-long preoccupations of Wilde.

Brian Hodgkiss

NOTES

1. Richard Ellmann: *Oscar Wilde* (Harmondsworth: Penguin, 1988), pp. 150-1.
2. Ibid. p. 173.
3. Ibid. p. 173.
4. Hesketh Pearson: *The Life of Oscar Wilde* (Harmondsworth: Penguin, 1950), p. 73.
5. Ibid. p. 84.
6. Walter Pater: letter to Wilde, 12 June, 1888.
7. *Athenaeum*, September 1888.
8. Ellmann, op. cit. p. 297.
9. Isobel Murray (ed), "Introduction" to *Oscar Wilde Complete Shorter Fiction* (Oxford: Oxford University Press, 1979), p. 10.
10. Ibid. p. 8.
11. Ellmann, op. cit. p. 240.
12. H. Montgomery Hyde: *Oscar Wilde: Plays, Prose and Poems* (Orbis Publishing Limited, 1982; Macdonald and Company Limited, 1989).
13. Murray, op. cit. p. 12.

Etching of Wilde and a child, possibly the artist's son,
by James Edward Kelly, 1882.

Chronology

1854	Born in Dublin 16 October 1854, the son of Sir William Wilde, a famous eye and ear specialist, and Jane Elgee, an Irish poet noted for her nationalism.
1864-71	Attends Portora Royal School in Enniskillen as a boarder.
1871-4	Wins a scholarship to Trinity College, Dublin, where he reads classics. Wins the Berkeley Gold Medal for Greek.
1874	Wins a Demyship (scholarship) in classics at Magdalen College, Oxford.
1874-8	Undergraduate at Oxford.
1874	Meets Ruskin, a major influence on his thinking.
1875	Visits Italy with John Pentland Mahaffy.
1876	Death of Sir William Wilde.
1877	Visits Greece with Mahaffy. Stops first at Ravenna. Visits Rome on returning from Greece.
1877	Is rusticated from April to October. Meets Walter Pater, a major influence in the development of Wilde's aestheticism.
1878	Wins the Newdigate Prize for his poem *Ravenna*. Takes double first

		in Greats (classics and philosophy). Moves to London; soon establishes himself as a wit.
1880		Privately prints his first play *Vera.*
1881		*Poems* published. Received with considerable hostility by the *Athenaeum*, the *Saturday Review*, the *Spectator* and *Punch*, but gains some support from friends.
1882		Lecture tour of the United States. Propagates the doctrine of aestheticism.
1882-3		Completes his second play, *The Duchess of Padua.* Not performed until 1891.
1883		*Vera* given its first performance in New York. Unfavourably received. Lecture tour in the United Kingdom. Lectures include "The House Beautiful", "Impressions of America", and "The Value of Art in Modern Life".
1884	**29 May**	Married to Constance Lloyd.
1885		Moves to 16 Tite Street, Chelsea. House redecorated by Edward Godwin. Wilde and Godwin want the house to set new standards in interior design.
	5 June	Birth of first son, Cyril.
1886		Meets Robert Ross at Oxford. Ross, having seduced Wilde, becomes first his lover and later his life-long friend.

	5 November	Birth of second son, Vyvyan.
1887-8		Edits *Woman's World.* Wants to make it "the organ of women of intellect, culture and position".
1888		*The Happy Prince and Other Tales* published. His reputation as an author dates from this book. Pater pays the compliment of saying the book is written in "pure English".
1889		Publishes *The Portrait of Mr W.H.* in *Blackwood's Magazine*. In it he advances the idea that Shakespeare wrote his sonnets for a boy actor, William Hughes.
1890	**20 June**	*The Picture of Dorian Gray* published in *Lippincott's Monthly Magazine.* "After this date Victorian literature had a different look." (Ellmann) The novel aroused much criticism and controversy, but Wilde answered his critics by claiming that art has nothing to do with morality.
1891		Meets Lord Alfred Douglas. *The Duchess of Padua* (under the title *Guido Ferranti*) performed in New York. Is badly received. *A House of Pomegranates* – which includes "The Birthday of the Infanta" – published.
	February	"The Soul of Man under Socialism" published.
	April	Publication of *Dorian Gray* in book form, with additions and a preface.
	May	*Intentions* published.

	July	*Lord Arthur Saville's Crime and Other Stories* published.
	November / December	Writes most of *Salomé* in French.
1892	**20 February**	First performance of *Lady Windermere's Fan* at the St. James's Theatre, London. Though it was a great public success, the response of the critics was less favourable. Wilde was accused of plagiarism, of constructing an improbable, even impossible, plot and of making all his male characters talk like himself – in paradoxes.
	June	Banning by the Lord Chamberlain of performance of *Salomé* on the English stage.
	August / September	Rents house in Norfolk and works on *A Woman of No Importance*. Invites Alfred Douglas to visit him. Finishes play.
1893	**February**	*Salomé* published, in French.
	19 April	First night of *A Woman of No Importance* at the Haymarket. Though the play was another public success, the reviews were mixed. *The Times* reviewer, however, wrote: "The play is fresh in ideas and execution and is written, moreover, with a literary polish too rare on the English stage", and William Archer described one scene (between Lord Illingworth and Mrs Arbuthnot at the end of Act II) as "the most

		virile and intelligent piece of English play-writing of our day".
1893-4		Finishes *An Ideal Husband.*
1894		Lord Alfred Douglas's translation of *Salomé* published. It was illustrated by Aubrey Beardsley. Wilde spends time with Douglas in Florence and in Brighton.
1895	**3 January**	First night of *An Ideal Husband.*
	January / February	Wilde in Algeria with Douglas. Meets André Gide.
	14 February	First night of *The Importance of Being Earnest* at the St. James's Theatre. The play was another public success and received a number of favourable critical notices.
	3 April	Trial of Lord Queensbury, Lord Alfred Douglas's father, for libel against Wilde.
	5 April	Queensbury acquitted. Wilde arrested for committing indecent acts.
	26 April – 1 May	Wilde's first trial. He praises the beauty and nobility of the "Love that dare not speak its name". A new trial is ordered because the jury fails to reach a verdict.
	20-25 May	The second trial. Wilde is sentenced to two years' imprisonment with hard labour for immorality and indecent behaviour.
	4 July	Wilde transferred from Pentonville, where he had been imprisoned in May, to Wandsworth Prison.

	20 November	Transferred to Reading Gaol, where he serves the rest of his sentence.
	September / November	Two bankruptcy trials. After the second, all Wilde's property put up for auction.
1896	**3 February**	Death of Lady Wilde.
1897		Writes a long letter to Douglas, later to be published as *De Profundis*.
	19 May	Released from prison. During his imprisonment, Wilde suffered physically, emotionally and mentally. His mother died, he was separated from his wife and denied further contact with his children. Through the writing of *De Profundis*, he seems to have achieved some kind of consolation and, he claims, the discovery of Christ.
	26 May	Goes to live in Berneval-sur-Mer, under the name of Sebastian Melmoth. Writes *The Ballad of Reading Gaol.*
	August	Reunion with Douglas, at Rouen. This was Wilde's second fall.
	September / December	With Douglas in Paris, Naples and Sicily.
	2 December	Douglas leaves Wilde in Naples. It is the end of the affair.
1898	**9 February**	Publication by Leonard Smithers of *The Ballad of Reading Gaol.*

	13 February	Returns from Naples to Paris and takes a room in a cheap hotel, the Hôtel de Nice.
	7 April	Death of Constance. Wilde is now living at the Hôtel d'Alsace, which will be his final address.
	June / July	Visits Nogent-sur-Marne.
	August	Goes to Chennièvres.
	15 December	Visits Napoule, near Cannes, as a guest of Frank Harris.
1899		*The Importance of Being Earnest* published in a limited edition, with revisions by Wilde.
	February	Visits Gland, in Switzerland, as the guest of Harold Mellors.
	1 April	Settles in Santa Margherita, on the Ligurian coast.
	July	*An Ideal Husband* published.
1900	**June**	Returns to Paris after travels in Italy. Takes a room at the Hôtel d'Alsace. Drinks heavily.
	Late September	Wilde is bedridden.
	10 October	Operation on his ear.
	16 October	Arrival in Paris of Ross on Wilde's birthday. Ross remains until Wilde's death.
	23 November	Dies at the Hôtel d'Alsace.
	3 December	Burial at Bagneux.

A Note on the Activities

In suggesting activities for this book, I did not want to keep exactly the same format for activities on each of the stories. I did, nevertheless, constantly bear a number of things in mind. First, I was aware of the problem of the wide range of vocabulary in Wilde's work and therefore glossed a large number of words. It is important, however, that students of a language should develop the habit of guessing the meanings of words through the contexts in which they occur. I have, therefore, included a number of exercises in which the student is asked to guess the meaning of words according to their contexts.

The activities to be done during reading are intended to ensure a general comprehension and sometimes to draw the student's attention to points of detail regarding character, setting, story and description. More subtle matters, such as shifts of feeling and tone, authorial comments, and some lexical, narrative and structural features are usually placed in the post-reading sections.

Something I have constantly borne in mind is the need to introduce ways of looking critically at a text. Here my predominant concerns have been with:

- **a.** *the art of narrative, the ways in which a story may have been told;*
- **b.** *the degree to which the author is present in the text [clearly related to **a**];*
- **c.** *the function of symbolism;*
- **d.** *the kind of characterisation to be observed in a story;*
- **e.** *stylistic elements;*
- ***f.*** *the tone of a story and its genre (comic, satirical, etc.);*
- **g.** *the use of linguistic devices such as simile, metaphor, inversion.*

It is hoped that the exercises suggested will result in a development both of linguistic ability and critical awareness. Any critical technique learnt here, it goes without saying, can be applied to any narrative text in any language.

It would be possible for a student working alone to benefit from the activities, but the help of a teacher is in general taken for granted. Many of the activities would be suitable for discussion in pairs or small groups, while others are more suitable for writing. The stories need not, of course, be read in the order in which they appear in the book, nor is it assumed that every single question will be answered. However, systematically working through the activities will result in a considerable understanding of Wilde as well as providing students with a number of ways of approaching a narrative text.

We must remember that we are reading stories by a highly individual writer. My first aim has been to help readers to appreciate and enjoy the unique flavour of these tales, so characteristic of their author in their gentleness and humour. The activities, therefore, are designed primarily to encourage an alert reading of the stories which will deepen enjoyment of them; but they may also, I hope, enhance future pleasures to be gained from reading other works of literature.

B.H.

Short Stories

 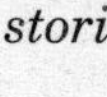

These symbols indicate the beginning and end of the three stories recorded on the cassette.

The Canterville Ghost

I

WHEN Mr Hiram B. Otis, the American Minister, bought Canterville Chase, every one told him he was doing a very foolish thing, as there was no doubt at all that the place was haunted. Indeed, Lord Canterville himself, who was a man of the most punctilious[1] honour, had felt it his duty to mention the fact to Mr Otis when they came to discuss terms.

'We have not cared to live in the place ourselves,' said Lord Canterville, 'since my grand-aunt, the Dowager Duchess[2] of Bolton, was frightened into a fit, from which she never really recovered, by two skeleton hands being placed on her shoulders as she was dressing for dinner, and I feel bound to tell you, Mr Otis, that the ghost has been seen by several living members of my family, as well as by the rector of the parish,[3] the Rev. Augustus Dampier, who is a Fellow[4] of King's College, Cambridge. After the unfortunate accident to the Duchess, none of our younger servants would stay with us, and Lady Canterville often got

1. *punctilious* [pʌŋk'tɪlɪəs] : correct, scrupulous.
2. *Dowager* ['daʊədʒər] *Duchess* : a woman holding the rank of duchess because her dead husband was a duke.
3. *parish* : an area within a diocese having its own church and clergyman.
4. *Fellow* : member of the governing body of a college.

very little sleep at night, in consequence of the mysterious noises that came from the corridor and the library.'

'My Lord,' answered the Minister, 'I will take the furniture and the ghost at a valuation. I come from a modern country, where we have everything that money can buy; and with all our spry [1] young fellows painting the Old World red,[2] and carrying off your best actors and prima-donnas, I reckon [3] that if there were such a thing as a ghost in Europe, we'd have it at home in a very short time in one of our public museums, or on the road as a show.'

'I fear that the ghost exists,' said Lord Canterville, smiling, 'though it may have resisted the overtures of your enterprising impresarios. It has been well known for three centuries, since 1584 in fact, and always makes its appearance before the death of any member of our family.'

'Well, so does the family doctor for that matter, Lord Canterville. But there is no such thing, sir, as a ghost, and I guess [4] the laws of Nature are not going to be suspended for the British aristocracy.'

'You are certainly very natural in America,' answered Lord Canterville, who did not quite understand Mr Otis's last observation, 'and if you don't mind a ghost in the house, it is all right. Only you must remember I warned you.'

A few weeks after this, the purchase was concluded, and at the close of the season the Minister and his family went down to Canterville Chase. Mrs Otis, who,

1. *spry* : active, lively.
2. *painting the Old World red*: "to paint the town red" is to have a boisterous time in the bars and nightclubs, etc. of a town. Wilde transfers the idiom to the whole of the Old World, *i.e.* Europe.
3. *reckon* (infml): think.
4. *guess* (American English): think.

as Miss Lucretia R. Tappen, of West 53rd Street, had been a celebrated New York belle, was now a very handsome,[1] middle-aged woman, with fine eyes, and a superb profile. Many American ladies on leaving their native land adopt an appearance of chronic ill-health, under the impression that it is a form of European refinement, but Mrs Otis had never fallen into this error. She had a magnificent constitution, and a really wonderful amount of animal spirits. Indeed, in many respects, she was quite English, and was an excellent example of the fact that we have really everything in common with America nowadays, except, of course, language. Her eldest son, christened Washington by his parents in a moment of patriotism, which he never ceased to regret, was a fair-haired, rather good-looking young man, who had qualified himself for American diplomacy by leading the German[2] at the Newport Casino for three successive seasons, and even in London was well known as an excellent dancer. Gardenias and the peerage[3] were his only weaknesses. Otherwise he was extremely sensible. Miss Virginia E. Otis was a little girl of fifteen, lithe[4] and lovely as a fawn,[5] and with a fine freedom in her large blue eyes. She was a wonderful amazon,[6] and had once raced old Lord Bilton on her pony twice round the park, winning by a length and a half, just in front of

1. *handsome* : used normally to describe a man but an older woman who remains good-looking in a striking way can be described as "handsome".
2. *German* : a dance.
3. *peerage* ['pɪərɪdʒ] : nobility.
4. *lithe* : flexible.
5. *fawn* : young deer.
6. *amazon* : tall strong athletic woman (from the Amazons in Greek mythology).

the Achilles statue, to the huge[1] delight of the young Duke of Cheshire, who proposed for her[2] on the spot, and was sent back to Eton that very night by his guardians, in floods of tears. After Virginia came the twins, who were usually called 'The Stars and Stripes,' as they were always getting swished.[3] They were delightful boys, and with the exception of the worthy[4] Minister the only true republicans of the family.

As Canterville Chase is seven miles from Ascot, the nearest railway station, Mr Otis had telegraphed for a waggonette[5] to meet them, and they started on their drive in high spirits. It was a lovely July evening, and the air was delicate with the scent of the pinewoods. Now and then they heard a wood pigeon brooding over its own sweet voice,[6] or saw, deep in the rustling fern,[7] the burnished[8] breast of the pheasant. Little squirrels peered at them from the beech-trees as they went by, and the rabbits scudded away through the brushwood[9] and over the mossy knolls,[10] with their white tails in the air. As they entered the avenue of Canterville

1. *huge* : enormous, immense.
2. *proposed for her* : asked to marry her.
3. *the twins . . . always getting swished* : "to be swished" means to be beaten with a cane, so that the red marks made by the cane on the twins were like the stars and stripes. "The Stars and Stripes" is the name of the American flag, so this is a play on words.
4. *worthy* ['wɜːði] : deserving respect.
5. *waggonette* : four-wheeled carriage.
6. *brooding over its own sweet voice* : thinking sadly about its sweet voice, presumably because one day the voice will fade or because it is singing a sad love song.
7. *rustling fern* : the fern is a plant with feathery green leaves which make a gentle noise when blown by a breeze.
8. *burnished* ['bɜːnɪʃt] : shiny.
9. *brushwood* : small trees and shrubs; undergrowth.
10. *knolls* [nəʊlz] : small hills.

Chase, however, the sky became suddenly overcast with[1] clouds, a curious stillness seemed to hold the atmosphere, a great flight of rooks[2] passed silently over their heads, and, before they reached the house, some big drops of rain had fallen.

Standing on the steps to receive them was an old woman, neatly dressed in black silk, with a white cap and apron. This was Mrs Umney, the housekeeper, whom Mrs Otis, at Lady Canterville's earnest[3] request, had consented to keep on in her former position. She made them each a low curtsey[4] as they alighted, and said in a quaint,[5] old-fashioned manner, 'I bid you welcome[6] to Canterville Chase.' Following her, they passed through the fine Tudor hall into the library, a long, low room, panelled in black oak,[7] at the end of which was a large stained-glass window.[8] Here they found tea laid out for them, and, after taking off their wraps,[9] they sat down and began to look round, while Mrs Umney waited on them.

Suddenly Mrs Otis caught sight of a dull red stain on the floor just by the fireplace and, quite unconscious of what it really signified, said to Mrs Umney, 'I am afraid something has been spilt there'

'Yes, madam,' replied the old housekeeper in a low voice, 'blood has been spilt on that spot.'

1. *overcast with* : made dark by.
2. *rooks* : large black birds of the crow family.
3. *earnest* ['ɜːnɪst] : serious, solemn.
4. *curtsey* ['kɜːtsi] : a salutation made by bending the knees and lowering the body.
5. *quaint* : odd, unusual.
6. *I bid you welcome* : I wish you welcome.
7. *panelled in black oak*: with walls covered in panels of dark oak wood.
8. *stained-glass window* : window of coloured glass, as in a church.
9. *wraps* [ræps] : outer clothes.

'How horrid,' cried Mrs Otis; 'I don't at all care for blood-stains in a sitting-room. It must be removed at once.'

The old woman smiled, and answered in the same low, mysterious voice, 'It is the blood of Lady Eleanore de Canterville, who was murdered on that very spot by her own husband, Sir Simon de Canterville, in 1575. Sir Simon survived her nine years, and disappeared suddenly under very mysterious circumstances. His body has never been discovered, but his guilty spirit still haunts the Chase. The blood-stain has been much admired by tourists and others, and cannot be removed.'

'That is all nonsense,' cried Washington Otis; 'Pinkerton's Champion Stain Remover and Paragon Detergent[1] will clean it up in no time,' and before the terrified housekeeper could interfere he had fallen upon his knees, and was rapidly scouring the floor with a small stick of what looked like a black cosmetic. In a few moments no trace of the blood-stain could be seen.

'I knew Pinkerton would do it,' he exclaimed triumphantly, as he looked round at his admiring family; but no sooner had he said these words than a terrible flash of lightning lit up the sombre[2] room, a fearful peal of thunder[3] made them all start to their feet, and Mrs Umney fainted.[4]

1. *Pinkerton's . . . Detergent* : in this story Wilde satirises American patent medicines and compounds. He refers here to a famous detective, Allan Pinkerton, but contemporary readers would also have been reminded of Lydia Pinkham, whose "medicinal compound" had been advertised on the same page as Wilde's portrait in the *Washington Post,* in 1882. (Wilde was in America at that time delivering lectures.) There is a song about Lydia Pinkham, "Lily the Pink".
2. *sombre* ['sɒmbər] : dark.
3. *peal of thunder* : loud burst of thunder.
4. *fainted* : lost consciousness.

'What a monstrous climate!' said the American Minister calmly, as he lit a long cheroot.[1] 'I guess the old country is so over-populated that they have not enough decent weather for everybody. I have always been of opinion that emigration is the only thing for England.'

'My dear Hiram,' cried Mrs Otis, 'what can we do with a woman who faints?'

'Charge it to her like breakages,'[2] answered the Minister, 'she won't faint after that;' and in a few moments Mrs Umney certainly came to.[3] There was no doubt, however, that she was extremely upset,[4] and she sternly[5] warned Mr Otis to beware of[6] some trouble coming to the house.

'I have seen things with my own eyes, sir,' she said, 'that would make any Christian's hair stand on end, and many and many a night I have not closed my eyes in sleep for the awful things that are done here.' Mr Otis, however, and his wife warmly assured the honest soul that they were not afraid of ghosts, and, after invoking the blessings of Providence on her new master and mistress, and making arrangements for an increase of salary, the old housekeeper tottered off to her own room.

1. *cheroot* [ʃəˈruːt] : cigar with both ends open.
2. *Charge it to her like breakages* : if a servant broke something, the cost of the item would be deducted from his/her pay. Mr Otis suggests a deduction should be made from Mrs Umney's pay because, while she is unconscious, she cannot work.
3. *came to* : regained consciousness.
4. *upset* : disturbed emotionally.
5. *sternly* : severely.
6. *beware* [bɪˈweər] *of* : be careful about.

II

THE STORM raged[1] fiercely all that night, but nothing of particular note occurred. The next morning, however, when they came down to breakfast, they found the terrible stain of blood once again on the floor. 'I don't think it can be the fault of the Paragon Detergent,' said Washington, 'for I have tried it with everything. It must be the ghost.' He accordingly[2] rubbed out the stain a second time, but the second morning it appeared again. The third morning also it was there, though the library had been locked up at night by Mr Otis himself, and the key carried upstairs. The whole family were now quite interested; Mr Otis began to suspect that he had been too dogmatic in his denial of the existence of ghosts, Mrs Otis expressed her intention of joining the Psychical Society,[3] and Washington prepared a long letter to Messrs. Myers and Podmore on the subject of the Permanence of Sanguineous Stains when connected with Crime. That night all doubts about the objective existence of phantasmata[4] were removed for ever.

1. *raged* : continued violently.
2. *accordingly* : for this reason.
3. *Psychical Society* : would be concerned with contacting the dead.
4. *phantasmata* : plural of "phantasma": ghosts, ghostly appearances.

The day had been warm and sunny; and, in the cool of the evening, the whole family went out to drive. They did not return home till nine o'clock, when they had a light supper. The conversation in no way turned upon ghosts, so there were not even those primary conditions of receptive expectation which so often precede the presentation of psychical phenomena. The subjects discussed, as I have since learned from Mr Otis, were merely such as form the ordinary conversation of cultured Americans of the better class, such as the immense superiority of Miss Fanny Davenport[1] over Sara Bernhardt as an actress; the difficulty of obtaining green corn, buckwheat cakes,[2] and hominy,[3] even in the best English houses; the importance of Boston[4] in the development of the world-soul; the advantages of the baggage check system in railway travelling; and the sweetness of the New York accent as compared to the London drawl.[5] No mention at all was made of the supernatural, nor was Sir Simon de Canterville alluded to in any way. At eleven o'clock the family retired, and by half-past all the lights were out. Some time after, Mr Otis was awakened by a curious noise in the corridor, outside his room. It sounded like the clank[6] of metal, and seemed to be coming nearer every moment. He got up

1. *Miss Fanny Davenport* : an actress much admired in America in the 1880s, but not generally considered comparable to Sara Bernhardt, who was much more famous.
2. *buckwheat cakes* : "buckwheat" is a plant, the flour of which is used to make cakes in America. Its seeds are used to feed animals in Europe.
3. *hominy* (American): ground maize.
4. *Boston* : Wilde is satirising the cultural pretensions of Boston.
5. *drawl* : a slow, lazy manner of speaking.
6. *clank* : used to describe the sound of metal striking something.

at once, struck a match, and looked at the time. It was exactly one o'clock. He was quite calm, and felt his pulse, which was not at all feverish.[1] The strange noise still continued, and with it he heard distinctly the sound of footsteps. He put on his slippers, took a small oblong phial[2] out of his dressing-case, and opened the door. Right in front of him he saw, in the wan[3] moonlight, an old man of terrible aspect. His eyes were as red burning coals; long grey hair fell over his shoulders in matted coils;[4] his garments, which were of antique cut, were soiled[5] and ragged, and from his wrists and ankles hung heavy manacles and rusty gyves.[6]

'My dear sir,' said Mr Otis, 'I really must insist on your oiling those chains, and have brought you for that purpose a mall bottle of the Tammany[7] Rising Sun Lubricator. It is said to be completely efficacious upon one application, and there are several testimonials to that effect on the wrapper[8] from some of our most eminent native divines. I shall leave it here for you by the bedroom candles, and will be happy to supply you with more should you require it.' With these words the United States Minister laid the bottle down on a marble table and, closing his door, retired to rest.

1. *feverish* : fast, as in a fever.
2. *phial* ['faɪəl] : small glass container.
3. *wan* [wɒn] : pale.
4. *matted coils* : the ghost's hair is twisted or entangled as if into pieces of rope.
5. *soiled* : dirty (past participle of "to soil": to make dirty).
6. *gyves* [dʒaɪvz] (now archaic): shackles for the legs (metal rings linked by a chain to restrict a prisoner's movements).
7. *Tammany* : the name of the central organization of the Democratic Party in the City (formerly also in the State) of New York. The Oxford English Dictionary says that in English the use of the word suggests political and municipal corruption. Wilde is again mocking American behaviour and ideals.
8. *wrapper* : paper in which the bottle is wrapped; perhaps the label.

For a moment the Canterville ghost stood quite motionless in natural indignation; then, dashing[1] the bottle violently upon the polished floor, he fled down the corridor, uttering[2] hollow groans, and emitting a ghastly[3] green light. Just, however, as he reached the top of the great oak staircase, a door was flung open, two little white-robed figures appeared, and a large pillow whizzed[4] past his head! There was evidently no time to be lost, so, hastily adopting the Fourth Dimension of Space as a means of escape, he vanished through the wainscoting,[5] and the house became quite quiet.

On reaching a small secret chamber in the left wing, he leaned up against a moonbeam to recover his breath, and began to try and realise his position. Never, in a brilliant and uninterrupted career of three hundred years, had he been so grossly insulted. He thought of the Dowager Duchess, whom he had frightened into a fit as she stood before the glass in her lace and diamonds; of the four housemaids, who had gone off into hysterics when he merely grinned at them through the curtains of one of the spare bedrooms; of the rector of the parish, whose candle he had blown out as he was coming late one night from the library, and who had been under the care of Sir William Gull ever since, a perfect martyr to nervous disorders; and of old Madame de Tremouillac, who, having wakened up one morning early and seen a skeleton seated in an armchair by the fire reading her diary, had been confined to her bed for six weeks with an attack of brain fever, and, on her recovery, had become

1. *dashing* : throwing.
2. *uttering*: emitting, giving voice to.
3. *ghastly* : causing terror or horror; death-like.
4. *whizzed* : moved very fast.
5. *wainscoting* ['weɪnskətɪŋ]: wooden covering on walls, especially on the lower half.

reconciled to the Church, and broken off her connection with that notorious sceptic Monsieur de Voltaire.[1] He remembered the terrible night when the wicked Lord Canterville was found choking in his dressing-room, with the knave of diamonds half-way down his throat, and confessed, just before he died, that he had cheated Charles James Fox out of £ 50,000 at Crockford's by means of that very card, and swore that the ghost had made him swallow it. All his great achievements came back to him again, from the butler[2] who had shot himself in the pantry because he had seen a green hand tapping at the window pane, to the beautiful Lady Stutfield, who was always obliged to wear a black velvet band round her throat to hide the mark of five fingers burnt upon her white skin, and who drowned herself at last in the carp-pond[3] at the end of the King's Walk. With the enthusiastic egotism of the true artist he went over his most celebrated performances, and smiled bitterly to himself as he recalled to mind his last appearance as 'Red Reuben, or the Strangled Babe,' his *début* as 'Gaunt Gibeon, the Blood-sucker of Bexley Moor,' and the *furore* he had excited one lovely June evening by merely playing ninepins[4] with his own bones upon the lawn-tennis ground. And after all this, some wretched modern Americans were to come and offer him the Rising Sun Lubricator, and throw pillows at his head! It was quite unbearable. Besides, no ghost in history had ever been treated in this manner. Accordingly, he determined to have vengeance and remained till daylight in an attitude of deep thought.

1. *Voltaire* (1694-1778): was sceptical about and satirised traditional religious and philosophical ideas.
2. *butler* : head manservant.
3. *carp-pond* : a "carp" is a large edible freshwater fish that lives in lakes or ponds.
4. *ninepins* : a game in which a ball is rolled along the ground with the object of knocking down nine bottle-shaped pieces of wood.

III

THE NEXT MORNING, when the Otis family met at breakfast they discussed the ghost at some length. The United States Minister was naturally a little annoyed to find that his present had not been accepted. 'I have no wish,' he said, 'to do the ghost any personal injury, and I must say that considering the length of time he has been in the house, I don' t think it is at all polite to throw pillows at him' – a very just remark, at which, I am sorry to say, the twins burst into shouts of laughter. 'Upon the other hand,' he continued, 'if he really declines to use the Rising Sun Lubricator, we shall have to take his chains from him. It would be quite impossible to sleep, with such a noise going on outside the bedrooms.'

For the rest of the week, however, they were undisturbed, the only thing that excited any attention being the continual renewal of the blood-stain on the library floor. This certainly was very strange, as the door was always locked at night by Mr Otis, and the windows kept closely barred. The chameleon-like colour, also, of the stain excited a good deal of comment. Some mornings it was a dull (almost Indian) red,[1] then it would be vermilion, then a rich purple, and once when they came down for family prayers, according to

1. *Indian red* : reddish brown colour like the skin of a Red Indian.

the simple rites of the Free American Reformed Episcopalian Church[1] they found it a bright emerald-green. These kaleidoscopic changes naturally amused the party very much, and bets on the subject were freely made every evening. The only person who did not enter into the joke was little Virginia, who, for some unexplained reason, was always a good deal distressed at the sight of the blood-stain, and very nearly cried the morning it was emerald-green.

The second appearance of the ghost was on Sunday night. Shortly after they had gone to bed they were suddenly alarmed by a fearful crash in the hall. Rushing downstairs they found that a large suit of old armour had become detached from its stand, and had fallen on the stone floor, while, seated in a high-backed chair, was the Canterville ghost, rubbing his knees with an expression of acute agony on his face. The twins, having brought their pea-shooters[2] with them, at once discharged two pellets on him, with that accuracy of aim which can only be attained by long and careful practice on a writing-master, while the United States Minister covered him with his revolver, and called upon him, in accordance with Californian etiquette, to hold up his hands! The ghost started up with a wild shriek[3] of rage, and swept through them like a mist, extinguishing Washington Otis's candle as he passed, and so leaving them all in total darkness. On reaching the top of the staircase he recovered himself, and determined to give his

1. *Episcopalian* [ɪˌpɪskəˈpeɪljən] *Church* : church governed by bishops, like the Church of England or the American church referred to here.
2. *pea-shooters* : tubes through which dried peas are shot by blowing. (Other things like balls of paper may be used instead of dried peas.)
3. *shriek* : scream, high-pitched cry.

celebrated peal [1] of demoniac laughter. This he had on more than one occasion found extremely useful. It was said to have turned Lord Raker's wig grey in a single night, and had certainly made three of Lady Canterville's French governesses give warning before their month was up. He accordingly laughed his most horrible laugh, till the old vaulted roof rang and rang again, but hardly had the fearful echo died away when a door opened, and Mrs Otis came out in a light blue dressing-gown. 'I am afraid you are far from well,' she said, 'and have brought you a bottle of Dr Dobell's tincture.[2] If it is indigestion, you will find it a most excellent remedy.' The ghost glared at her in fury, and began at once to make preparations for turning himself into a large black dog, an accomplishment for which he was justly renowned, and to which the family doctor always attributed the permanent idiocy of Lord Canterville's uncle, the Hon. Thomas Horton. The sound of approaching footsteps, however, made him hesitate in his fell [3] purpose, so he contented himself with becoming faintly phosphorescent, and vanished with a deep churchyard groan,[4] just as the twins had come up to him.

On reaching his room he entirely broke down, and became a prey to [5] the most violent agitation. The vulgarity of the twins, and the gross materialism of Mrs Otis, were naturally extremely annoying, but what really distressed him most was, that he had been unable to wear the suit of mail.[6] He had hoped that

1. *peal* : burst (as of thunder, for example).
2. *tincture* ['tɪŋktʃər] : medicine.
3. *fell* : fierce, destructive.
4. *churchyard groan* : a frightening deep sound made when in pain ("churchyards" are associated with terror).
5. *a prey to* : a victim of.
6. *mail* : armour.

even modern Americans would be thrilled by the sight of a Spectre In Armour, if for no more sensible reason, at least out of respect for their national poet Longfellow,[1] over whose graceful and attractive poetry he himself had whiled away many a weary hour when the Cantervilles were up in town. Besides, it was his own suit. He had worn it with great success at the Kenilworth tournament, and had been highly complimented on it by no less a person than the Virgin Queen[2] herself. Yet when he had put it on, he had been completely overpowered by the weight of the huge breastplate and steel casque,[3] and had fallen heavily on the stone pavement, barking[4] both his knees severely, and bruising the knuckles of his right hand.

For some days after this he was extremely ill, and hardly stirred out of his room at all, except to keep the blood-stain in proper repair. However, by taking great care of himself, he recovered, and resolved to make a third attempt to frighten the United States Minister and his family. He selected Friday, the 17th of August, for his appearance, and spent most of that day in looking over his wardrobe, ultimately deciding in favour of a large slouched hat[5] with a red feather, a winding-sheet[6] frilled[7] at the wrists and neck, and a rusty dagger. Towards evening a violent storm of rain came on, and the wind was so high that all the windows and doors in the old house shook and rattled.

1. *Longfellow* (1807-82) : the American poet, wrote a story called "The Skeleton in Armour" (1841). His most famous work is *Hiawatha*.
2. *Virgin Queen* : Elizabeth I (1533-1603).
3. *casque* : helmet.
4. *barking* : injuring by scraping.
5. *slouched* [slaʊtʃt] *hat* : a hat with a wide flexible brim.
6. *winding-sheet* ['waɪndɪŋ ʃiːt] : a sheet in which a corpse is wrapped for burial.
7. *frilled* : with frills (decorative borders).

In fact, it was just such weather as he loved. His plan of action was this. He was to make his way quietly to Washington Otis's room, gibber[1] at him from the foot of the bed, and stab himself three times in the throat to the sound of low music. He bore Washington a special grudge, being quite aware that it was he who was in the habit of removing the famous Canterville blood-stain, by means of Pinkerton's Paragon Detergent. Having reduced the reckless and foolhardy[2] youth to a condition of abject terror, he was then to proceed to the room occupied by the United States Minister and his wife, and there to place a clammy[3] hand on Mrs Otis's forehead, while he hissed[4] into her trembling husband's ear the awful secrets of the charnel-house.[5] With regard to little Virginia, he had not quite made up his mind. She had never insulted him in any way, and was pretty and gentle. A few hollow groans from the wardrobe, he thought, would be more than sufficient, or, if that failed to wake her, he might grabble at the counterpane[6] with palsy-twitching[7] fingers. As for the twins, he was quite determined to teach them a lesson. The first thing to be done was, of course, to sit upon their chests, so to produce the stifling[8] sensation of nightmare. Then, as

1. *gibber* : speak fast and inarticulately, chatter like an ape.
2. *reckless and foolhardy* : two words that reinforce each other – they mean "careless of danger".
3. *clammy* : cold and moist.
4. *hissed* (onomatopoeic): made sharp sibilant sound like a snake.
5. *charnel-house* : house or vault where dead bodies are piled.
6. *grabble at the counterpane* : feel for, reach his hands towards, the bedspread (cover for the bed).
7. *palsy-twitching* ['pɔːlzi twɪtʃɪŋ] : moving convulsively as if suffering with palsy, a disease characterised by involuntary tremors.
8. *stifling* ['staɪflɪŋ] : producing a sensation of deprivation of breath.

their beds were quite close to each other, to stand between them in the form of a green, icy-cold corpse, till they became paralysed with fear, and finally, to throw off the winding-sheet, and crawl round the room, with white, bleached[1] bones and one rolling eyeball, in the character of 'Dumb Daniel, or the Suicide's Skeleton,' a *rôle* in which he had on more than one occasion produced a great effect, and which he considered quite equal to his famous part of 'Martin the Maniac, or the Masked Mystery.'

At half-past ten he heard the family going to bed. For some time he was disturbed by wild shrieks of laughter from the twins, who, with the light-hearted gaiety of schoolboys, were evidently amusing themselves before they retired to rest, but at a quarter past eleven all was still, and, as midnight sounded, he sallied forth.[2] The owl beat against the window panes, the raven croaked from the old yew-tree,[3] and the wind wandered moaning round the house like a lost soul; but the Otis family slept unconscious of their doom,[4] and high above the rain and storm he could hear the steady snoring of the Minister for the United States. He stepped stealthily out of the wainscoting, with an evil smile on his cruel, wrinkled mouth, and the moon hid her face in a cloud as he stole past the great oriel window,[5] where his own arms[6] and those of his murdered wife were blazoned[7] in azure and gold.

1. *bleached* : whitened, made white.
2. *sallied forth* : went out, started out.
3. *yew-tree* : an evergreen dark-leaved coniferous tree, often planted in graveyards.
4. *doom* : terrible fate.
5. *oriel* ['ɔːrɪəl] *window* : projecting window, normally on an upper floor.
6. *arms* : coat of arms, heraldic devices of a family – often in the form of a shield.
7. *blazoned* ['bleɪznd] : painted.

On and on he glided,[1] like an evil shadow, the very darkness seeming to loathe him[2] as he passed. Once he thought he heard something call, and stopped; but it was only the baying[3] of a dog from the Red Farm, and he went on, muttering strange sixteenth-century curses, and ever and anon[4] brandishing the rusty dagger in the midnight air. Finally he reached the comer of the passage that led to luckless Washington's room. For a moment he paused there, the wind blowing his long grey locks about his head, and twisting into grotesque and fantastic folds the nameless horror of the dead man's shroud.[5] Then the clock struck the quarter, and he felt the time was come. He chuckled[6] to himself, and turned the corner, but no sooner had he done so, than, with a piteous wail[7] of terror, he fell back, and hid his blanched[8] face in his long, bony hands. Right in front of him was standing a horrible spectre, motionless as a carven[9] image, and monstrous as a madman's dream! Its head was bald and burnished; its face round, and fat, and white; and hideous laughter seemed to have writhed its features into an eternal grin. From the eyes streamed rays of scarlet light, the mouth was a wide well of fire, and a hideous garment, like to his own, swathed with its silent snows the Titan form. On its

1. *glided* : moved noiselessly and smoothly.
2. *loathe him* : regard him with disgust.
3. *baying* : barking, howling.
4. *ever and anon* : occasionally.
5. *shroud* : sheet in which corpses are wrapped (same as winding sheet).
6. *chuckled* : made a suppressed sound of laughter.
7. *wail* : sound of lament.
8. *blanched* : whitened.
9. *carven* : cut out of wood; carved.

breast was a placard[1] with strange writing in antique characters, some scroll[2] of shame it seemed, some record of wild sins, some awful calendar of crime, and, with its right hand, it bore aloft a falchion[3] of gleaming steel.

Never having seen a ghost before, he naturally was terribly frightened, and, after a second hasty[4] glance at the awful phantom, he fled back to his room, tripping up[5] in his long winding sheet as he sped down the corridor, and finally dropping the rusty dagger into the Minister's jack-boots,[6] where it was found in the morning by the butler. Once in the privacy of his own apartment, he flung himself down on a small pallet-bed,[7] and hid his face under the clothes. After a time, however, the brave old Canterville spirit asserted itself, and he determined to go and speak to the other ghost as soon as it was daylight. Accordingly, just as the dawn was touching the hills with silver, he returned towards the spot where he had first laid eyes on the grisly[8] phantom, feeling that, after all, two ghosts were better than one, and that, by the aid of his new friend, he might safely grapple with the twins. On reaching the spot, however, a terrible sight met his gaze. Something had evidently happened to the spectre, for the light had entirely faded from its hollow eyes, the gleaming falchion had fallen from its hand, and it was leaning up against the wall in a strained

1. *placard* : sheet written on like a poster.
2. *scroll* : roll of parchment or paper; here, design imitating the form of a scroll.
3. *falchion* ['fɔːltʃən] : a type of sword.
4. *hasty* : quick, hurried.
5. *tripping up* : stumbling, almost falling.
6. *jack-boots* : large boots coming above the knee.
7. *pallet-bed* : straw bed; mattress.
8. *grisly* ['grɪzli] : causing horror.

and uncomfortable attitude. He rushed forward and seized it in his arms, when, to his horror, the head slipped off and rolled on the floor, the body assumed a recumbent posture, and he found himself clasping a white dimity[1] bedcurtain, with a sweeping-brush, a kitchen cleaver,[2] and a hollow turnip[3] lying at his feet! Unable to understand this curious transformation, he clutched the placard with feverish haste, and there, in the grey morning light, he read these fearful words:-

YE OTIS GHOSTE.[4]
Ye Onlie True and Originale Spook.
Beware of Ye Imitationes.
All others are Counterfeite.

The whole thing flashed across him.[5] He had been tricked, foiled,[6] and outwitted! The old Canterville look came into his eyes; he ground[7] his toothless gums together, and, raising his withered[8] hands high above his head, swore, according to the picturesque phraseology of the antique school, that when Chanticleer[9] had sounded twice his merry horn, deeds

1. *dimity* ['dɪmɪti] : type of cotton fabric with raised stripes or squares.
2. *cleaver*: a chopper for cutting meat.
3. *turnip* : a type of root vegetable.
4. *YE OTIS GHOSTE:* this and the rest of the words on the placard are spelt in a pseudo-archaic manner. The use of "ye" instead of "the" and of forms like "onlie" and "Imitationes" represents the twins' naive idea of archaic English.
5. *flashed across him* : suddenly came to him.
6. *foiled* : defeated; frustrated.
7. *ground* : rubbed together hard (past tense of "to grind").
8. *withered* ['wɪðəd] : dried up.
9. *Chanticleer* : the name given to the cockerel by Chaucer in his tale "Chanticleer and Partlet".

of blood would be wrought, and Murder walk abroad with silent feet.

Hardly had he finished this awful oath[1] when, from the red-tiled roof of a distant homestead, a cock crew. He laughed a long, low, bitter laugh, and waited. Hour after hour he waited, but the cock, for some strange reason, did not crow again. Finally, at half-past seven, the arrival of the housemaids made him give up his fearful vigil, and he stalked[2] back to his room, thinking of his vain oath and baffled[3] purpose. There he consulted several books of ancient chivalry, of which he was exceedingly fond, and found that, on every occasion on which this oath had been used, Chanticleer had always crowed a second time. 'Perdition seize the naughty fowl,' he muttered, 'I have seen the day when, with my stout spear, I would have run him through the gorge,[4] and made him crow for me an 'twere[5] in death!' He then retired to a comfortable lead coffin, and stayed there till evening.

1. *oath* : a solemn promise in the name of God or some revered or dreaded person.
2. *stalked* : walked in a very definite, presumably angry manner.
3. *baffled* : defeated, frustrated.
4. *'Perdition . . . fowl' . . . run him through the gorge* : This is an example of Wilde's literary parody from *Othello* "Perdition catch my soul / But I do love thee"; Gray's "The Bard": "Ruin seize thee, ruthless King!" and from *King Lear:* "I have seen the day, with my good biting falchion / I would have made them skip." Note Wilde's earlier use of "falchion" (p. 26, note 3). "Gorge" – another Shakespearean word – means throat.
5. *an 'twere* : as if it were.

OTIS GHOST

IV

THE NEXT DAY the ghost was very weak and tired. The terrible excitement of the last four weeks was beginning to have its effect. His nerves were completely shattered,[1] and he started[2] at the slightest noise. For five days he kept his room, and at last made up his mind to give up the point of the blood-stain on the library floor. If the Otis family did not want it, they clearly did not deserve it. They were evidently people on a low, material plane of existence, and quite incapable of appreciating the symbolic value of sensuous phenomena. The question of phantasmic apparitions, and the development of astral bodies,[3] was of course quite a different matter, and really not under his control. It was his solemn duty to appear in the corridor once a week, and to gibber from the large oriel window on the first and third Wednesdays in every month, and he did not see how he could honourably escape from his obligations. It is quite true that his life had been very evil, but, upon the other hand, he was most conscientious in all things connected with the supernatural. For the next three Saturdays, accordingly, he traversed the corridor as usual

1. *shattered* : broken into small pieces, destroyed.
2. *started* : made sudden nervous movements.
3. *astral bodies* : stars.

between midnight and three o'clock, taking every possible precaution against being either heard or seen. He removed his boots, trod[1] as lightly as possible on the old worm-eaten boards, wore a large black velvet cloak, and was careful to use the Rising Sun Lubricator for oiling his chains. I am bound to acknowledge that it was with a good deal of difficulty that he brought himself to adopt this last mode of protection. However, one night, while the family were at dinner, he slipped into Mr Otis's bedroom and carried off the bottle. He felt a little humiliated at first, but afterwards was sensible enough to see that there was a great deal to be said for the invention, and, to a certain degree, it served his purpose. Still, in spite of everything, he was not left unmolested. Strings were continually being stretched across the corridor, over which he tripped in the dark, and on one occasion, while dressed for the part of 'Black Isaac, or the Huntsman of Hogley Woods,' he met with a severe fall, through treading on a butter-slide,[2] which the twins had constructed from the entrance of the Tapestry Chamber to the top of the oak staircase. This last insult so enraged him, that he resolved to make one final effort to assert his dignity and social position, and determined to visit the insolent young Etonians the next night in his celebrated character of 'Reckless Rupert, or the Headless Earl.'

He had not appeared in this disguise for more than seventy years: in fact, not since he had so frightened pretty Lady Barbara Modish[3] by means of it, that she

1. *trod* : stepped, walked.
2. *treading on a butter-slide* : stepping on a very slippery track made by the twins, who had put butter on the floor and stairs, sliding on it to make it more slippery.
3. *Lady Barbara Modish* : the name suggests she was very fashionable.

suddenly broke off her engagement with the present Lord Canterville's grandfather, and ran away to Gretna Green with handsome Jack Castletown, declaring that nothing in the world would induce her to marry into a family that allowed such a horrible phantom to walk up and down the terrace at twilight. Poor Jack was afterwards shot in a duel by Lord Canterville on Wandsworth Common, and Lady Barbara died of a broken heart at Tunbridge Wells before the year was out, so, in every way, it had been a great success. It was, however, an extremely difficult 'make-up,'[1] if I may use such a theatrical expression in connection with one of the greatest mysteries of the supernatural, or, to employ a more scientific term, the higher-natural world, and it took him fully three hours to make his preparations. At last everything was ready, and he was very pleased with his appearance. The big leather riding-boots that went with the dress were just a little too large for him, and he could only find one of the two horse-pistols,[2] but, on the whole, he was quite satisfied, and at a quarter past one he glided out of the wainscoting and crept down the corridor. On reaching the room occupied by the twins, which I should mention was called the Blue Bed Chamber, on account of the colour of its hangings,[3] he found the door just ajar.[4] Wishing to make an effective entrance, he flung it[5] wide open, when a heavy jug of water fell right down on him, wetting him to the skin, and just missing his left shoulder by a couple of

1. *'make-up'* : refers here to the use of make-up on the stage to transform people's appearance.
2. *horse-pistols* : pistols for use by horsemen.
3. *hangings* : pieces of cloth hunging on the walls as a form of decoration; tapestry.
4. *ajar* : a little open.
5. *flung it* : threw it vigorously.

inches. At the same moment he heard stifled shrieks of laughter proceeding from the four-post bed.[1] The shock to his nervous system was so great that he fled back to his room as hard as he could go, and the next day he was laid up with a severe cold. The only thing that at all consoled him in the whole affair was the fact that he had not brought his head with him, for, had he done so, the consequences might have been very serious.

He now gave up all hope of ever frightening this rude American family, and contented himself, as a rule, with creeping about the passages in list slippers,[2] with a thick red muffler[3] round his throat for fear of draughts, and a small arquebuse,[4] in case he should be attacked by the twins. The final blow he received occurred on the 19th of September. He had gone downstairs to the great entrance-hall, feeling sure that there, at any rate, he would be quite unmolested, and was amusing himself by making satirical remarks on the large Saroni[5] photographs of the United States Minister and his wife, which had now taken the place of the Canterville family pictures. He was simply but neatly clad in a long shroud, spotted with churchyard mould,[6] had tied up his jaw[7] with a strip of yellow linen, and carried a small lantern and a sexton's spade. In fact, he was dressed for the character of 'Jonas the Graveless, or the Corpse-Snatcher of

1. *four-post bed* : a bed with four posts supporting a canopy.
2. *list slippers* : slippers made out of pieces cut from the edges of cloth.
3. *muffler* : scarf.
4. *arquebuse* (now *harquebus* or *arquebus*): an early type of portable gun.
5. *Saroni* : American photographer who took photographs of celebrities, including, in 1882, Wilde himself.
6. *mould* [məʊld]: earth.
7. *tied up his jaw* : as he is dead, to prevent it from dropping open.

Chertsey Barn,' one of his most remarkable impersonations, and one which the Cantervilles had every reason to remember, as it was the real origin of their quarrel with their neighbour, Lord Rufford. It was about a quarter past two o'clock in the morning, and, as far as he could ascertain, no one was stirring. As he was strolling towards the library, however, to see if there were any traces left of the blood-stain, suddenly there leaped out on him from a dark corner two figures, who waved their arms wildly above their heads, and shrieked out 'BOO!' [1] in his ear.

Seized with a panic, which, under the circumstances, was only natural, he rushed for the staircase, but found Washington Otis waiting for him there with the big garden-syringe; [2] and bang thus hemmed in [3] by his enemies on every side, and driven almost to bay, he vanished into the great iron stove, which, fortunately for him, was not lit, and had to make his way home through the flues [4] and chimneys, arriving at his own room in a terrible state of dirt, disorder, and despair.

After this he was not seen again on any nocturnal expedition. The twins lay in wait for him on several occasions, and strewed the passages with nutshells [5] every night to the great annoyance of their parents and the servants, but it was of no avail. It was quite evident that his feelings were so wounded that he would not appear. Mr Otis consequently resumed his great work on the history of the Democratic Party, on

1. *'BOO!'*: used to surprise or startle someone.
2. *garden-syringe* : a garden-spray.
3. *hemmed in* : surrounded.
4. *flues* : channels for smoke in a chimney.
5. *strewed the passage with nutshells* : the twins scattered nutshells in the passage to make the ghost slip and fall.

which he had been engaged for some years; Mrs Otis organised a wonderful clam-bake,[1] which amazed the whole county; the boys took to lacrosse, euchre, poker,[2] and other American national games; and Virginia rode about the lanes on her pony, accompanied by the young Duke of Cheshire, who had come to spend the last week of his holidays at Canterville Chase. It was generally assumed that the ghost had gone away, and, in fact, Mr Otis wrote a letter to that effect to Lord Canterville, who, in reply, expressed his great pleasure at the news, and sent his best congratulations to the Minister's worthy wife.

The Otises, however, were deceived, for the ghost was still in the house, and though now almost an invalid, was by no means ready to let matters rest, particularly as he heard that among the guests was the young Duke of Cheshire, whose grand-uncle, Lord Francis Stilton, had once bet a hundred guineas with Colonel Carbury that he would play dice with the Canterville ghost, and was found the next morning lying on the floor of the card-room in such a helpless paralytic state, that though he lived on to a great age, he was never able to say anything again but 'Double Sixes.' The story was well known at the time, though, of course, out of respect to the feelings of the two noble families, every attempt was made to hush it up;[3] and a full account of all the circumstances connected with it will be found in the third volume of Lord Tattle's[4] *Recollections of the Prince Regent and his Friends.* The ghost, then, was naturally very anxious to show that he had not lost his influence over the Stiltons, with

1. *clam-bake* : a party where clams (a type of mollusc) are cooked and eaten outdoors.
2. *euchre* ['juːkər], *poker* : American card games.
3. *hush it up* : keep it quiet, suppress the story.
4. *Lord Tattle* : "tattle" means "gossip".

whom, indeed, he was distantly connected, his own first cousin having been married *en secondes noces*[1] to the Sieur[2] de Bulkeley, from whom, as every one knows, the Dukes of Cheshire are lineally descended. Accordingly, he made arrangements for appearing to Virginia's little lover in his celebrated impersonation of 'The Vampire Monk, or, the Bloodless Benedictine,' a performance so horrible that when old Lady Startup[3] saw it, which she did on one fatal New Year's Eve, in the year 1764, she went off into the most piercing shrieks, which culminated in violent apoplexy, and died in three days, after disinheriting the Cantervilles, who were her nearest relations, and leaving all her money to her London apothecary.[4] At the last moment, however, his terror of the twins prevented his leaving his room, and the little Duke slept in peace under the great feathered canopy in the Royal Bedchamber, and dreamed of Virginia.

1. *en secondes noces* : in a second marriage.
2. *Sieur* : Master.
3. *Lady Startup* : another name suggesting the character of the person.
4. *apothecary* [əˈpɒθəkəri] (archaic): chemist.

V

A FEW DAYS after this, Virginia and her curly-haired cavalier went out riding on Brockley meadows, where she tore her habit [1] so badly in getting through a hedge, that, on their return home, she made up her mind to go up by the back staircase so as not to be seen. As she was running past the Tapestry Chamber,[2] the door of which happened to be open, she fancied [3] she saw some one inside, and thinking it was her mother's maid, who sometimes used to bring her work there, looked in to ask her to mend her habit. To her immense surprise, however, it was the Canterville Ghost himself! He was sitting by the window, watching the ruined gold of the yellowing trees fly through the air, and the red leaves [4] dancing madly down the long avenue. His head was leaning on his hand, and his whole attitude was one of extreme depression. Indeed, so forlorn, and so much out of repair did he look, that little Virginia, whose

1. *habit* (archaic): coat.
2. *Tapestry Chamber* : a room with tapestries hanging on the walls.
3. *fancied* : imagined.
4. "*ruined gold . . . red leaves*" : this is again literary parody. The "ruined gold" comes from Tennyson's *Maud* (l. 12) and the dancing "red leaves" from Coleridge's *Christabel* (ll. 48-50).

first idea had been to run away and lock herself in her room, was filled with pity, and determined to try and comfort him. So light was her footfall, and so deep his melancholy, that he was not aware of her presence till she spoke to him.

'I am so sorry for you,' she said, 'but my brothers are going back to Eton to-morrow, and then, if you behave yourself, no one will annoy you.'

'It is absurd asking me to behave myself,' he answered looking round in astonishment at the pretty little girl who had ventured to address him, 'quite absurd. I must rattle my chains,[1] and groan through keyholes, and walk about at night, if that is what you mean. It is my only reason for existing.'

'It is no reason at all for existing, and you know you have been very wicked. Mrs Umney told us, the first day we arrived here, that you had killed your wife.'

'Well, I quite admit it,' said the Ghost petulantly, 'but it was a purely family matter, and concerned no one else.'

'It is very wrong to kill any one.' said Virginia, who at times had a sweet Puritan gravity, caught from some old New England ancestor.[2]

'Oh, I hate the cheap severity of abstract ethics! My wife was very plain,[3] never had my ruffs[4] properly starched,[5] and knew nothing about cookery. Why,

1. *rattle my chains* : cause his chains to make short, sharp metallic noises as they strike against each other.
2. *New England ancestor* : when the Puritans emigrated to America, they settled in the north-eastern states of Maine, New Hampshire, Vermont, Massachusetts, Rhode Island and Connecticut. The region came to be known as New England.
3. *plain* : the opposite of pretty, not exactly ugly, but very ordinary in looks.
4. *ruffs* : a ruff is a frill of starched linen or muslin worn round the neck. You can see them in pictures of the Elizabethan period.
5. *starched* : made stiff with starch, which is prepared from carbohydrates.

there was a buck[1] I had shot in Hogley Woods, a magnificent pricket,[2] and do you know how she had it sent up to table? However, it is no matter now, for it is all over, and I don't think it was very nice of her brothers to starve me to death, though I did kill her.'

'Starve you to death? Oh, Mr Ghost, I mean Sir Simon, are you hungry? I have a sandwich in my case. Would you like it?'

'No, thank you, I never eat anything now; but it is very kind of you, all the same, and you are much nicer than the rest of your horrid, rude, vulgar, dishonest family.'

'Stop!' cried Virginia stamping her foot, 'it is you who are rude, and horrid, and vulgar, and as for dishonesty, you know you stole the paints out of my box to try and furbish up[3] that ridiculous blood-stain in the library. First you took all my reds, including the vermilion, and I couldn't do any more sunsets, then you took the emerald-green and the chrome-yellow, and finally I had nothing left but indigo and Chinese white, and could only do moonlight scenes, which are always depressing to look at, and not at all easy to paint. I never told on you, though I was very much annoyed, and it was most ridiculous, the whole thing; for who ever heard of emerald-green blood?'

'Well, really,' said the Ghost, rather meekly,[4] 'what was I to do? It is a very difficult thing to get real blood nowadays, and, as your brother began it all with his Paragon Detergent, I certainly saw no reason why I should not have your paints. As for colour, that is always a matter of taste: the Cantervilles have

1. *buck* : male deer.
2. *pricket* [prıkıt]: a two-year old male deer.
3. *furbish up* : renew.
4. *meekly* : humbly, submissively.

blue blood,[1] for instance, the very bluest in England; but I know you Americans don't care for things of this kind.'

'You know nothing about it, and the best thing you can do is to emigrate and improve your mind. My father will be only too happy to give you a free passage, and though there is a heavy duty[2] on spirits of every kind, there will be no difficulty about the Custom House, as the officers are all Democrats. Once in New York, you are sure to be a great success. I know lots of people there who would give a hundred thousand dollars to have a grandfather,[3] and much more than that to have a family ghost.'

'I don't think I should like America.'

'I suppose because we have no ruins and no curiosities,' said Virginia satirically.

'No ruins! no curiosities!' answered the Ghost; 'you have your navy and your manners.'

'Good evening; I will go and ask papa to get the twins an extra week's holiday.'

'Please don't go, Miss Virginia,' he cried; 'I am so lonely and so unhappy, and I really don't know what to do. I want to go to sleep and I cannot.'

'That's quite absurd! You have merely to go to bed and blow out the candle. It is very difficult sometimes to keep awake, especially at church, but there is no difficulty at all about sleeping. Why, even babies know how to do that, and they are not very clever.'

'I have not slept for three hundred years,' he said sadly, and Virginia's beautiful blue eyes opened in

1. *blue blood* : aristocrats were said to have blue blood. "To have blue blood" is to be of aristocratic descent.
2. *duty* : a tax on some imported goods, like spirits.
3. *to have a grandfather* : Wilde is making fun of Americans, who, aware that their country was young and without long family traditions, were concerned to establish for themselves even a recent ancestry.

wonder; 'for three hundred years I have not slept, and I am so tired.'

Virginia grew quite grave,[1] and her little lips trembled like rose-leaves. She came towards him, and kneeling down at his side, looked up into his old withered face.

'Poor, poor Ghost,' she murmured; 'have you no place where you can sleep?'

'Far away beyond the pinewoods,' he answered, in a low dreamy voice, 'there is a little garden. There the grass grows long and deep, there are the great white stars of the hemlock[2] flower, there the nightingale sings all night long. All night long he sings, and the cold, crystal moon looks down, and the yew-tree spreads out its giant arms over the sleepers.'

Virginia's eyes grew dim with tears, and she hid her face in her hands.

'You mean the Garden of Death,' she whispered.

'Yes, Death. Death must be so beautiful. To lie in the soft brown earth, with the grasses waving above one's head, and listen to silence. To have no yesterday, and no to-morrow. To forget time, to forgive life, to be at peace. You can help me. You can open for me the portals of Death's house, for Love is always with you, and Love is stronger than Death[3] is.'

Virginia trembled, a cold shudder[4] ran through her, and for a few moments there was silence. She felt as if she was in a terrible dream.

Then the Ghost spoke again, and his voice sounded like the sighing of the wind.

1. *grave* : serious.
2. *hemlock* : a poisonous plant with pretty flowers.
3. *Love is stronger than Death* : Wilde uses the words of the Authorized Version of the Bible here, e.g. The Song of Solomon 8:6, 7.
4. *shudder* : a shiver of fear or horror.

'Have you ever read the old prophecy on the library window?'

'Oh, often,' cried the little girl, looking up; 'I know it quite well. It is painted in curious black letters, and it is difficult to read. There are only six lines:

When a golden girl can win
Prayer from out the lips of sin,
When the barren[1] *almond bears,*
And a little child gives away its tears,
Then shall all the house be still
And peace come to Canterville.

But I don't know what they mean.'

'They mean,' he said sadly, 'that you must weep with me for my sins, because I have no tears, and pray with me for my soul, because I have no faith, and then, if you have always been sweet, and good, and gentle, the Angel of Death will have mercy on me. You will see fearful shapes in darkness, and wicked voices will whisper in your ear, but they will not harm you, for against the purity of a little child the powers of Hell cannot prevail.'

Virginia made no answer, and the Ghost wrung his hands[2] in wild despair as he looked down at her bowed golden head. Suddenly she stood up, very pale, and with a strange light in her eyes. 'I am not afraid,' she said firmly, 'and I will ask the Angel to have mercy on you.'

He rose from his seat with a faint cry of joy, and taking her hand bent over it with old-fashioned grace and kissed it. His fingers were as cold as ice, and his lips burned like fire, but Virginia did not falter, as he

1. *barren* : infertile.
2. *wrung his hands* : squeezed his hands in distress (here the distress of despair).

led her across the dusky room. On the faded green tapestry were broidered[1] little huntsmen. They blew their tasselled[2] horns and with their tiny hands waved to her to go back. 'Go back! little Virginia,' they cried, 'go back!' but the Ghost clutched[3] her hand more tightly, and she shut her eyes against them. Horrible animals with lizard tails, and goggle eyes,[4] blinked at her from the carven chimney-piece, and murmured 'Beware! little Virginia, beware! we may never see you again,' but the Ghost glided on more swiftly, and Virginia did not listen. When they reached the end of the room he stopped, and muttered some words she could not understand. She opened her eyes, and saw the wall slowly fading away like a mist, and a great black cavern in front of her. A bitter cold wind swept round them, and she felt something pulling at her dress. 'Quick, quick,' cried the Ghost, 'or it will be too late,' and, in a moment, the wainscoting had closed behind them, and the Tapestry Chamber was empty.

1. *broidered* : embroidered, decorated with needlework.
2. *tasselled* ['tæsld] : with tassels (bunches of threads tied at one end and hanging as ornaments from cushions, caps and, in this case, horns).
3. *clutched* : held, grasped.
4. *goggle eyes* : full, protuberant eyes.

VI

ABOUT ten minutes later, the bell rang for tea, and, as Virginia did not come down, Mrs Otis sent up one of the footmen[1] to tell her. After a little time he returned and said that he could not find Miss Virginia anywhere. As she was in the habit of going out to the garden every evening to get flowers for the dinner-table, Mrs Otis was not at all alarmed at first, but when six o'clock struck, and Virginia did not appear, she became really agitated, and sent the boys out to look for her, while she herself and Mr Otis searched every room in the house. At half-past six the boys came back and said that they could find no trace of their sister anywhere. They were all now in the greatest state of excitement, and did not know what to do, when Mr Otis suddenly remembered that, some few days before, he had given a band of gipsies permission to camp in the park. He accordingly at once set off for Blackfell Hollow, where he knew they were, accompanied by his eldest son and two of the farm-servants. The little Duke of Cheshire, who was perfectly frantic with anxiety, begged hard to be allowed to go too, but Mr Otis would not allow him, as he was afraid there might be a scuffle.[2] On arriving

1. *footmen* : servants (wearing livery, a kind of uniform).
2. *scuffle* : struggle, fight.

at the spot, however, he found that the gipsies had gone, and it was evident that their departure had been rather sudden, as the fire was still burning, and some plates were lying on the grass. Having sent off Washington and the two men to scour[1] the district, he ran home, and despatched telegrams to all the police inspectors in the country, telling them to look out for a little girl who had been kidnapped by tramps[2] or gipsies. He then ordered his horse to be brought round, and, after insisting on his wife and the three boys sitting down to dinner, rode off down the Ascot road with a groom.[3] He had hardly, however, gone a couple of miles, when he heard somebody galloping after him, and, looting round, saw the little Duke coming up on his pony, with his face very flushed[4] and no hat. 'I'm awfully sorry, Mr Otis,' gasped out the boy, 'but I can't eat any dinner as long as Virginia is lost. Please, don't be angry with me; if you had let us be engaged last year, there would never have been all this trouble. You won't send me back, will you? I can't go! I won't go!'

The Minister could not help smiling at the handsome young scapegrace,[5] and was a good deal touched at his devotion to Virginia, so leaning down from his horse, he patted him kindly on the shoulders, and said, 'Well, Cecil, if you won't go back I suppose you must come with me, but I must get you a hat at Ascot.'

'Oh, bother my hat! I want Virginia!' cried the little Duke, laughing, and they galloped on to the railway

1. *scour* ['skaʊər]: search.
2. *tramps* : vagabonds.
3. *groom* : person in charge of horses.
4. *flushed* : reddened.
5. *scapegrace* : a person who is often in trouble because of a wild, impetuous or thoughtless character.

station. There Mr Otis inquired of the station-master if any one answering to the description of Virginia had been seen on the platform, but could get no news of her. The station-master, however, wired up and down the line, and assured him that a strict watch would be kept for her, and, after having bought a hat for the little Duke from a linen-draper,[1] who was just putting up his shutters,[2] Mr Otis rode off to Bexley, a village about four miles away, which he was told was a well-known haunt[3] of the gipsies, as there was a large common next to it. Here they roused up[4] the rural policeman, but could get no information from him, and, after riding all over the common, they turned their horses' heads homewards, and reached the Chase about eleven o'clock, dead-tired and almost heartbroken. They found Washington and the twins waiting for them at the gate-house with lanterns, as the avenue was very dark. Not the slightest trace of Virginia had been discovered. The gipsies had been caught on Brockley meadows, but she was not with them, and they had explained their sudden departure by saying that they had mistaken the date of Chorton Fair, and had gone off in a hurry for fear they might be late. Indeed, they had been quite distressed at hearing of Virginia's disappearance, as they were very grateful to Mr Otis for having allowed them to camp in his park, and four of their number had stayed behind to help in the search. The carp-pond had been dragged,[5] and the whole Chase thoroughly gone over, but without any result. It was evident that, for that

1. *linen-draper* : seller of linen.
2. *shutters* : here wooden or metal panels acting as protection against thieves.
3. *haunt* : a place often frequented.
4. *roused up* : woke up.
5. *dragged* : searched (using nets, hooks, etc.).

night at any rate, Virginia was lost to them; and it was in a state of the deepest depression that Mr Otis and the boys walked up to the house, the groom following behind with the two horses and the pony. In the hall they found a group of frightened servants, and lying on a sofa in the library was poor Mrs Otis, almost out of her mind with terror and anxiety, and having her forehead bathed with eau-de-cologne by the old housekeeper. Mr Otis at once insisted on her having something to eat, and ordered up supper for the whole party. It was a melancholy meal, as hardly any one spoke, and even the twins were awestruck[1] and subdued, as they were very fond of their sister. When they had finished, Mr Otis, in spite of the entreaties[2] of the little Duke, ordered them all to bed, saying that nothing more could be done that night, and that he would telegraph in the morning to Scotland Yard for some detectives to be sent down immediately. Just as they were passing out of the dining-room, midnight began to boom[3] from the clock tower, and when the last stroke sounded they heard a crash and a sudden shrill[4] cry, a dreadful peal of thunder shook the house, a strain[5] of unearthly music floated through the air, a panel at the top of the staircase flew back with a loud noise, and out on the landing, looking very pale and white, with a little casket[6] in her hand, stepped Virginia. In a moment they had all rushed up to her. Mrs Otis clasped her

1. *awestruck* : struck with a sense of fear.
2. *entreaties* : pleas, requests.
3. *boom* : make a loud, echoing noise, like the striking of a church clock.
4. *shrill* : high-pitched.
5. *strain* : part of a piece of music.
6. *casket* : small box for jewels.

passionately in her arms, the Duke smothered[1] her with violent kisses, and the twins executed a wild war-dance round the group.

'Good heavens! child, where have you been?' said Mr Otis rather angrily, thinking that she had been playing some foolish trick on them. 'Cecil and I have been riding all over the country looking for you, and your mother has been frightened to death. You must never play these practical jokes any more.'

'Except on the Ghost! except on the Ghost!' shrieked the twins, as they capered about.[2]

'My own darling, thank God you are found; you must never leave my side again,' murmured Mrs Otis, as she kissed the trembling child, and smoothed the tangled gold of her hair.

'Papa,' said Virginia quietly, 'I have been with the Ghost. He is dead, and you must come and see him. He had been very wicked, but he was really sorry for all that he had done, and he gave me this box of beautiful jewels before he died.'

The whole family gazed at her in mute amazement, but she was quite grave and serious;[3] and, turning round, she led them through the opening in the wainscoting down a narrow secret corridor, Washington following with a lighted candle, which he had caught up from the table. Finally, they came to a great oak door, studded[4] with rusty nails. When Virginia touched it, it swung back on its heavy hinges, and they found themselves in a little low room, with

1. *smothered* : overwhelmed. "Smothered her with kisses" – gave her an excessive number of kisses.
2. *capered about* : jumped about (with joy).
3. *grave and serious* : synonyms, but "grave" suggests dignified seriousness.
4. *studded* : decorated (studs are large-headed nails or knobs used for decoration or ornament).

a vaulted ceiling,[1] and one tiny grated[2] window. Imbedded[3] in the wall was a huge iron ring, and chained to it was a gaunt[4] skeleton, that was stretched out at full length on the stone floor, and seemed to be trying to grasp with its long fleshless fingers an old-fashioned trencher[5] and ewer,[6] that were placed just out of its reach. The jug had evidently been once filled with water, as it was covered inside with green mould. There was nothing on the trencher but a pile of dust. Virginia knelt down beside the skeleton, and, folding her little hands together, began to pray silently, while the rest of the party looked on in wonder at the terrible tragedy whose secret was now disclosed to them.

'Hallo!' suddenly exclaimed one of the twins, who had been looking out of the window to try and discover in what wing of the house the room was situated. 'Hallo! the old withered almond-tree has blossomed. I can see the flowers quite plainly in the moonlight.'

'God has forgiven him,' said Virginia gravely, as she rose to her feet, and a beautiful light seemed to illumine her face.

'What an angel you are!' cried the young Duke, and he put his arm round her neck, and kissed her.

1. *vaulted ceiling* : ceiling in the shape of a vault, an arched ceiling.
2. *grated* : with metal bars across it.
3. *Imbedded* : deeply set.
4. *gaunt* : lean and grim.
5. *trencher* : wooden plate.
6. *ewer* [ˈjuːər] : water-jug.

VII

FOUR DAYS after these curious incidents a funeral started from Canterville Chase at about eleven o'clock at night. The hearse[1] was drawn by eight black horses, each of which carried on its head a great tuft[2] of nodding ostrich-plumes, and the leaden coffin was covered by a rich purple pall,[3] on which was embroidered in gold the Canterville coat-of-arms. By the side of the hearse and the coaches walked the servants with lighted torches, and the whole procession was wonderfully impressive. Lord Canterville was the chief mourner,[4] having come up specially from Wales to attend the funeral, and sat in the first 'carriage along with little Virginia. Then came the United States Minister and his wife, then Washington and the three boys, and in the last carriage was Mrs Umney. It was generally felt that, as she had been frightened by the ghost for more than fifty years of her life, she had a right to see the last of him. A deep grave had been dug in the corner of the churchyard, just under the old yew-tree, and the

1. *hearse* [hɜːs]: vehicle used to carry the coffin at a funeral.
2. *tuft* : bunch of feathers, held together at the base.
3. *pall* [pɔːl]: a cloth used to cover a coffin.
4. *mourner* : one who mourns, shows grief for the dead.

service was read in the most impressive manner by the Rev. Augustus Dampier. When the ceremony was over, the servants, according to an old custom observed in the Canterville family, extinguished their torches, and, as the coffin was being lowered into the grave, Virginia stepped forward, and laid on it a large cross made of white and pink almond-blossoms. As she did so, the moon came out from behind a cloud, and flooded with its silent silver the little churchyard, and from a distant copse a nightingale began to sing. She thought of the ghost's description of the Garden of Death, her eyes became dim with tears,[1] and she hardly spoke a word during the drive home.

The next morning, before Lord Canterville went up to town, Mr Otis had an interview with him on the subject of the jewels the ghost had given to Virginia. They were perfectly magnificent, especially a certain ruby necklace with old Venetian setting, which was really a superb specimen of sixteenth-century work, and their value was so great that Mr Otis felt considerable scruples about allowing his daughter to accept them.

'My lord,' he said, 'I know that in this country mortmain[2] is held to apply to trinkets[3] as well as to land, and it is quite clear to me that these jewels are, or should be, heirlooms[4] in your family. I must beg you, accordingly, to take them to London with you, and to regard them simply as a portion of your property which has been restored to you under certain

1. *her eyes became dim with tears* : she could not see because of the tears.
2. *mortmain* ['mɔːtmeɪn] : literally "dead hand"; legal term that refers to the condition of lands held as a right, here by the Canterville family.
3. *trinkets* : jewels, ornaments.
4. *heirlooms* : pieces of property owned by a family for generations.

strange conditions. As for my daughter, she is merely a child, and has as yet, I am glad to say, but little interest in such appurtenances[1] of idle luxury. I am also informed by Mrs Otis, who, I may say, is no mean authority[2] upon Art – having had the privilege of spending several winters in Boston when she was a girl – that these gems are of great monetary worth, and if offered for sale would fetch a tall price.[3] Under these circumstances, Lord Canterville, I feel sure that you will recognise how impossible it would be for me to allow them to remain in the possession of any member of my family; and, indeed, all such vain gauds and toys,[4] however suitable or necessary to the dignity of the British aristocracy, would be completely out of place among those who have been brought up on the severe, and I believe immortal, principles of Republican simplicity. Perhaps I should mention that Virginia is very anxious that you should allow her to retain the box, as a memento of your unfortunate but misguided ancestor. As it is extremely old, and consequently a good deal out of repair, you may perhaps think fit to comply with her request. For my own part, I confess I am a good deal surprised to find a child of mine expressing sympathy with mediævalism in any form, and can only account for it by the fact that Virginia was born in one of your London suburbs shortly after Mrs Otis had returned from a trip to Athens.'

Lord Canterville listened very gravely to the worthy Minister's speech, pulling his grey moustache now and

1. *appurtenances* [ə'pɜːtɪnənsɪz] : accessories.
2. *no mean authority* : a very good (here knowledgeable) authority.
3. *a tall price* : a high price.
4. *vain gauds* [veɪn gɔːdz] *and toys* : empty or insignificant ornaments and trivial things.

then to hide an involuntary smile, and when Mr Otis had ended, he shook him cordially by the hand, and said, 'My dear sir, your charming little daughter rendered my unlucky ancestor, Sir Simon, a very important service, and I and my family are much indebted to her for her marvellous courage and pluck.[1] The jewels are clearly hers, and, egad,[2] I believe that if I were heartless enough to take them from her, the wicked old fellow would be out of his grave in a fortnight, leading me the devil of a life. As for their being heirlooms, nothing is an heirloom that is not so mentioned in a will[3] or legal document, and the existence of these jewels has been quite unknown. I assure you have no more claim on them than your butler, and when Miss Virginia grows up I daresay[4] she will be pleased to have pretty things to wear. Besides, you forget, Mr Otis, that you took the furniture and the ghost at a valuation, and anything that belonged to the ghost passed at once into your possession, as, whatever activity Sir Simon may have shown in the corridor at night, in point of law he was really dead, and you acquired his property by purchase.'

Mr Otis was a good deal distressed at Lord Canterville's refusal, and begged him to reconsider his decision, but the good-natured peer was quite firm, and finally induced the Minister to allow his daughter to retain the present the ghost had given her, and when, in the spring of 1890, the young Duchess of Cheshire was presented at the Queen's first drawing-room[5] on the occasion of her marriage, her jewels were the universal theme of admiration. For Virginia received the coronet,

1. *pluck* : another word for "courage".
2. *egad* (archaic) : by God.
3. *will* : testament.
4. *I daresay* : it is very probable.
5. *drawing-room* : a room for the formal reception of visitors.

which is the reward of all good little American girls, and was married to her boy-lover as soon as he came of age. They were both so charming, and they loved each other so much, that every one was delighted at the match, except the old Marchioness of Dumbleton, who had tried to catch the Duke for one of her seven unmarried daughters, and had given no less than three expensive dinner-parties for that purpose, and, strange to say, Mr Otis himself. Mr Otis was extremely fond of the young Duke personally, but, theoretically, he objected to tides, and, to use his own words, 'was not without apprehension lest,[1] amid the enervating influences of a pleasure-loving aristocracy, the true principles of Republican simplicity should be forgotten.' His objections, however, were completely overruled, and I believe that when he walked up the aisle[2] of St. George's, Hanover Square, with his daughter leaning on his arm, there was not a prouder man in the whole length and breadth of England.

The Duke and Duchess, after the honeymoon was over, went down to Canterville Chase, and on the day after their arrival they walked over in the afternoon to the lonely churchyard by the pine-woods. There had been a great deal of difficulty at first about the inscription on Sir Simon's tombstone, but finally it had been decided to engrave[3] on it simply the initials of the old gentleman's name, and the verse from the library window. The Duchess had brought with her some lovely roses, which she strewed[4] upon the grave, and after they had stood by it for some time they

1. *lest* : for fear that.
2. *aisle* [aɪl] : the space between blocks of seats in a theatre, church, etc.
3. *engrave* : cut letters or a design into metal, stone, etc.
4. *strewed* [struːd] : scattered.

strolled[1] into the ruined chancel[2] of the old abbey. There the Duchess sat down on a fallen pillar, while her husband lay at her feet smoking a cigarette and looking up at her beautiful eyes. Suddenly he threw his cigarette away, took hold of her hand, and said to her, 'Virginia, a wife should have no secrets from her husband.'

'Dear Cecil! I have no secrets from you.'

'Yes, you have,' he answered, smiling, 'you have never told me what happened to you when you were locked up with the ghost.'

'I have never told any one, Cecil,' said Virginia gravely.

'I know that, but you might tell me.'

'Please don't ask me, Cecil, I cannot tell you. Poor Sir Simon! I owe him a great deal. Yes, don't laugh, Cecil, I really do. He made me see what Life is, and what Death signifies, and why Love is stronger than both.'

The Duke rose and kissed his wife lovingly.

'You can have your secret as long as I have your heart,' he murmured.

'You have always had that, Cecil.'

'And you will tell our children some day, won't you?'

Virginia blushed.

1. *strolled* : walked in a relaxed or leisurely way.
2. *chancel* : a part of a church, near the altar.

Pre-reading Activity

Thinking of the ghost stories you know, what do you expect in a ghost story? Write down your ideas in the grid below, after discussing them in pairs or small groups.

SETTING	
PERIOD	
ATMOSPHERE	
CHARACTERS	
EVENTS	
TYPES OF GHOST	

Activities while Reading

SECTION I

Read the first section of the story (pp. 5-12).

1. Wilde uses an immense range of vocabulary in this story. The notes explain a large number of words but it is valuable to guess meanings from their context. What do you think the following mean?

WORD	YOUR GUESS	DICTIONARY DEFINITION
haunted		
fit		
overtures		
floods (of tears)		
scudded away		
alighted		
scouring		
tottered off		

Now check your guesses in your monolingual dictionary and with your teacher. Always try to guess meanings according to context and consult your dictionary only after guessing.

2. What transaction is taking place between Mr Otis and Lord Canterville on the first page of the story?

3. Mr Otis and Lord Canterville have different views about the existence of ghosts. Can you say what they are?

4. Describe briefly the members of the Otis family.

MEMBER OF THE FAMILY	PHYSICAL CHARACTERISTICS, IF GIVEN	OTHER FEATURES
Mr Otis		
Mrs Otis		
Washington Otis		
Virginia Otis		
The twins		

5. Wilde suggests something ominous is about to happen as the Otis family approaches Canterville Chase. Show how he does this by completing the grid.

Weather before the family reaches Canterville Chase	**Weather as the family enters the avenue of Canterville Chase**

6. What details are given in the first description of Canterville Chase (p. 8, para. 2)?

7. What was the origin of the bloodstain and what is strange about it?

8. How does Washington demonstrate his lack of superstition?

9. How does Nature seem to respond to Washington's removal of the bloodstain?

10. What sort of story would you expect after this opening section? Choose from the following list of adjectives and give the reasons for your choices.

historical	frightening	supernatural	comical	tragic
satirical	contemporary	mysterious	suspenseful	romantic

Section II

1. What were the reactions of Mr Otis, Mrs Otis and Washington to the repeated reappearance of the bloodstain?

People	Reactions
Mr Otis	
Mrs Otis	
Washington	

2. Describe the ghost on its first appearance (p. 16).
3. Describe the ghost's flight.
4. Describe the ghost's past "performances". What happened to the people he had frightened?

People the Ghost had Frightened	The Ghost's Past "Performances"
The Dowager Duchess	
The four house-maids	
The Rector of the Parish	
Madame de Tremouillac	
Lord Canterville	
Lady Stutfield	

SECTION III

1. What is absurd about the Minister's remarks in the first paragraph?

2. Explain why the suit of armour had fallen to the ground and why the ghost was rubbing his knees.

3. How do the twins, Mr Otis and Mrs Otis behave when the ghost appears a second time? How is their behaviour different from that of people who had been haunted in the same way in the past? Complete the grid.

CHARACTERS	**BEHAVIOUR**	**DIFFERENCE**
Twins		
Mr Otis		
Mrs Otis		

4. Describe the ghost's feelings after his humiliating experience with the Otis family and the suit of armour. Complete the grid.

	THE GHOST'S FEELINGS
Towards the twins	
Towards Mrs Otis	
Towards the suit of armour	

5. How does the ghost next intend to frighten the various members of the Otis household? Complete the grid.

MEMBER OF THE FAMILY	THE GHOST'S PLAN
Washington Otis	
Mr and Mrs Otis	
Virginia	
The twins	

6. What descriptive details are given to suggest the atmosphere of fear as the ghost is about to haunt the family again? Complete the grid.

DESCRIPTIONS OF NATURE	
DESCRIPTION OF THE GHOST (movements, appearance, sounds)	

7. Describe the "horrible spectre" encountered by the ghost. Complete the grid.

HEAD, FACE AND EXPRESSION	
CLOTHES AND OTHER DETAILS	
GENERAL IMPRESSION	

8. Explain how the ghost had been tricked and his reaction to being tricked.

SECTION IV

1. In what state of mind is the ghost four weeks after the arrival of the Otis family at Canterville Chase?
2. How does the ghost's disguise as "Reckless Rupert," or the "Headless Earl" result in disaster for him and comedy for the twins?
3. What finally dissuaded the ghost from undertaking any nocturnal expeditions?

SECTION V

1. Read the description at the end of the section, where Virginia disappears with the ghost. What adjectives from the list below would you choose to describe the atmosphere here? Give reasons for your choice.

joyful	frightening	mysterious	comical
ominous	hopeful	suspicious	suspenseful

2. Virginia promises to ask the Angel of Death to have mercy on the ghost. How do you predict the story will end?

Section VI

1. What do you think has happened to Virginia?
2. Look at Wilde's description of the reappearance of Virginia. What use does Wilde make of noises and movement in this description?

Noises	
Movement	

3. What do the family find when Virginia leads them to the place of the ghost's death? Describe the scene in your own words.

Section VII

1. The description of the funeral is in general serious. Pick out a sentence that disturbs the serious tone.
2. Read Mr Otis's speech (pp. 52-3). How does he reveal his puritanical attitude?
3. The story ends: "Virginia blushed". Why do you think she blushed?
4. What is the moral of the story?

Post-reading Activities

Wilde's Language and Style

Comedy

Wilde was a great comic writer, particularly in his play *The Importance of Being Earnest*. In "The Canterville Ghost" there is considerable use of comedy, through which Wilde sometimes makes satirical points and at other times produces a sense of absurdity. Answer the following questions on aspects of Wilde's comedy.

1. Re-read page 6, paragraph 1. How does Wilde make fun of American attitudes here?

2. "I guess the laws of Nature are not going to be suspended for the British aristocracy" (p. 6, para. 3). Lord Canterville does not understand this remark of Mr Otis. What, in fact, does Mr Otis mean and in what way is he being ironical at the expense of the British aristocracy?

3. Re-read pages 6-7. According to Wilde, how did Mrs Otis differ from many other American ladies who came to settle in England? What is he satirising here?

4. "... we have really everything in common with America nowadays, except, of course, language." What is the point of Wilde's joke?

5. Read from "I knew Pinkerton would do it" (p. 11) to the end of the section. What comic point is Wilde making when he writes:
" ... after invoking the blessings of Providence on her new master and mistress, and making arrangements for an increase of salary, the old housekeeper tottered off to her own room".

6. How does Wilde make fun of "cultured Americans of the better class" on page 15 (Section II, para. 2)?

7. What is comical about the following?
  a. Mr Otis's first words to the ghost (p. 16);
  b. the ghost's oath (pp. 27-8);
  c. the ghost's motives for killing his wife (pp. 38-40).

8. Re-read the conversation between Virginia and the ghost (pp. 38-43), then answer the following questions:
  a. What satirical elements are there in the first part of the conversation (pp. 38-41)?
  b. In what way is Wilde's use of "spirits" (p. 41) a play on words?
  c. What horrible threat does Virginia make?
  d. When does the tone of the conversation change and what is the difference between its first half and its second?

Description

Wilde uses description principally to heighten the atmosphere of his story or to produce comic effects. Sometimes having heightened the atmosphere, he will deliberately deflate the effect. Find one example of:

  a. description used to heighten atmosphere;
  b. description used for comic effect;
  c. sudden comic deflation of apparently serious description

Similes

Wilde is fond of using effective similes. Look at page 24, para. 2. Find two similes and suggest their appropriateness in the context. Now read the last paragraph of Section V. Find and comment on the three similes.

Use of Natural Phenomena, Animals and Objects to Create Atmosphere

Read the paragraph beginning 'As Canterville Chase...' (pp. 8-9) and look at your answer to Section 1, Question 5. Pick out the examples of the use of nature, birds and animals to create an atmosphere.
Now turn again to page 24, para. 2. Describe the effect here of the description of animals, birds and natural phenomena.

Characterisation

1. Write a character sketch of your favourite character and say why you like this character best.

2. Which is the most comical character? Explain the reasons for your choice.

Narrative Technique

The four most frequently encountered narrative modes are:

a. Narration in the third person by a narrator who knows everything about the characters in a novel and what happened to them. Such a narrator can reproduce not only dialogues that occurred between characters but the inner thoughts of the characters. We call this type of narrator an omniscient narrator.

b. Third person narration in which the narrator identifies with one of the characters, seeing the action and other characters from the point of view of that one character. The narrator will pretend to have only a partial view of characters and events.

c. First person narration in which the narrator sees everything only from his or her point of view.

d. First person narration in which the narrator knows the other characters so well that his or her view of the action is almost omniscient.

There are, of course, many variations on these four basic models of narration: double narration, multiple narration, novels in which the narrator apparently almost disappears, novels in which characters and events are revealed mainly by letters, and so on.

When we think of the omniscient narrator, we can ask ourselves how obtrusive or unobtrusive he/she is. An obtrusive narrator is always telling us very directly what to think of characters and situations. Some of the very greatest novels, however, have very obtrusive narrators, for example, Tolstoy, in *War and Peace* or, to draw an example from English Literature, George Elliot, in *Middlemarch.*

1. How would you describe Wilde as a narrator in "The Canterville Ghost"?

2. How obtrusive/unobtrusive is he?

The Presence of Wilde in the Story

Read the paragraph beginning "A few weeks after this" on page 6. In what sentences do you feel Wilde speaks most directly? What is his purpose in intruding directly into the narrative in this way?
Now read the dialogue between the ghost and Virginia, (pp. 38-43). Virginia is given words that a girl of fifteen would be unlikely to say. Find examples of Wilde's intrusions into this dialogue. When you re-read the story, note how frequently Wilde intrudes into the narrative, usually to comic or satirical effect.

Themes

Which themes do you consider most important in this story? Give reasons for your answers.

- **a.** "Old World" manners and attitudes versus those of the "New World".
- **b.** Scepticism versus credulity.
- **c.** Redemption through love.
- **d.** The power of innocence and youth for good.
- **e.** The disrespect of the young for the old.

Can you think of any other themes in the story?

A Particular Characteristic of "The Canterville Ghost"

One amusing aspect of "The Canterville Ghost" is the names given to the Ghost's various disguises, e.g. "Red Reuben", or the "Strangled Babe", which conjures up an image of a red-haired, perhaps red-bearded villain who strikes fear into everybody who sees him. List the other disguises that the Ghost has adopted, making a comment on the image that each name creates.

Personal Response

1. Which aspects of this story did you enjoy most and why? Think, for example, of the comic and the sentimental elements in the story.

2. In the Pre-reading Activity you were asked to think of ghost stories that you know. Having read and studied "The Canterville Ghost", in what ways do you think it is different from conventional ghost stories?

The Happy Prince

HIGH above the city, on a tall column, stood the statue of the Happy Prince. He was gilded[1] all over with thin leaves of fine gold, for eyes he had two bright sapphires, and a large red ruby glowed[2] on his sword-hilt.[3]

He was very much admired indeed. 'He is as beautiful as a weathercock,'[4] remarked one of the Town Councillors who wished to gain a reputation for having artistic tastes; 'only not quite so useful,' he added, fearing lest people should think him unpractical,[5] which he really was not.

'Why can't you be like the Happy Prince?' asked a sensible mother of her little boy who was crying for the moon. 'The Happy Prince never dreams of crying for anything.'

'I am glad there is someone in the world who is quite happy,' muttered a disappointed man as he gazed at the wonderful statue.

1. *gilded* : covered with a thin layer of gold.
2. *glowed* [gləʊd] : shone with an intense light.
3. *sword-hilt* : handle of sword.
4. *weathercock* : a pointer, traditionally in the shape of a cock, usually mounted on a church spire, which shows the direction of the wind.
5. *fearing . . . unpractical* : "Lest" suggests he doesn't want people to think he is unpractical. Here we could substitute "in case".

'He looks just like an angel,' said the Charity Children[1] as they came out of the cathedral in their bright scarlet cloaks and their dean white pinafores.[2]

'How do you know?' said the Mathematical Master. 'You have never seen one.'

'Ah! but we have, in our dreams,' answered the children; and the Mathematical Master frowned[3] and looked very severe, for he did not approve of children dreaming.

One night there flew over the city a little Swallow.[4] His friends had gone away to Egypt six weeks before, but he had stayed behind, for he was in love with the most beautiful Reed.[5] He had met her early in the spring as he was flying down the river after a big yellow moth, and had been so attracted by her slender waist that he had stopped to talk to her.

'Shall I love you?' said the Swallow, who liked to come to the point at once, and the Reed made him a low bow.[6] So he flew round and round her, touching the water with his wings, and making silver ripples.[7] This was his courtship, and it lasted all through the summer.

'It is a ridiculous attachment,' twittered the other Swallows; 'she has no money, and far too many

1. *Charity Children* : children (often orphans) looked after by the state or by charitable organizations.
2. *pinafores* ['pɪnəfɔːz] : a washable covering worn over the dress to protect against dirt.
3. *frowned* [fraʊnd] : expressed displeasure ("to frown" is to bring one's eyebrows together, so making vertical wrinkles on the forehead. It is a sign of displeasure).
4. *Swallow* ['swɒləʊ] : a swift-flying, insectivorous, migratory bird.
5. *Reed* : a strong-stemmed water plant.
6. *bow* [baʊ] : bend at the waist as a sign of respect.
7. *ripples* : small waves.

relations'; and indeed the river was quite full of Reeds. Then, when the autumn came they all flew away.

After they had gone he felt lonely, and began to tire of his lady-love. 'She has no conversation,' he said, 'and I am afraid that she is a coquette,[1] for she is always flirting with the wind.' And certainly, whenever the wind blew, the Reed made the most graceful curtsies.[2] 'I admit that she is domestic,' he continued, 'but I love travelling, and my wife, consequently, should love travelling also.'

'Will you come away with me?' he said finally to her, but the Reed shook her head, she was so attached to her home.

'You have been trifling with me,'[3] he cried. 'I am off to the Pyramids. Good-bye!' and he flew away.

All day long he flew, and at night-time he arrived at the city. 'Where shall I put up?'[4] he said; 'I hope the town has made preparations.'

Then he saw the statue on the tall column.

'I will put up there,' he cried; 'it is a fine position, with plenty of fresh air.' So he alighted[5] just between the feet of the Happy Prince.

'I have a golden bedroom,' he said softly to himself as he looked round, and he prepared to go to sleep; but just as he was putting his head under his wing a large drop of water fell on him. 'What a curious thing!' he cried; 'there is not a single cloud in the sky, the stars are quite clear and bright, and yet it is raining. The climate in the north of Europe is really dreadful.

1. *coquette* : flirt.
2. *curtsies* ['kɜːtsɪz] : a woman or girl's salutation made by bending the knees and lowering the body.
3. *trifling with me* : treating me in a frivolous manner, without seriousness.
4. *put up* : lodge, find accommodation.
5. *alighted* : landed.

The Reed used to like the rain, but that was merely her selfishness.'

Then another drop fell.

'What is the use of a statue if it cannot keep the rain off?' he said; 'I must look for a good chimney-pot,' and he determined to fly away.

But before he had opened his wings, a third drop fell, and he looked up, and saw – Ah! what did he see?

The eyes of the Happy Prince were filled with tears, and tears were running down his golden cheeks. His face was so beautiful in the moonlight that the little Swallow was filled with pity.

'Who are you?' he said.

'I am the Happy Prince.'

'Why are you weeping then?' asked the Swallow; 'you have quite drenched me.'

'When I was alive and had a human heart,' answered the statue, 'I did not know what tears were, for I lived in the Palace of Sans-Souci,[1] where sorrow is not allowed to enter. In the day-time I played with my companions in the garden, and in the evening I led the dance in the Great Hall. Round the garden ran a very lofty wall, but I never cared to ask what lay beyond it, everything about me was so beautiful. My courtiers called me the Happy Prince, and happy indeed I was, if pleasure be[2] happiness. So I lived, and so I died. And now that I am dead they have set me up here so high that I can see all the ugliness and all the misery of my city, and though my heart is made of lead yet I cannot choose but weep.'

1. *the Palace of Sans-Souci* : the palace without care, where there are no cares.
2. *be* : is. "Be" is here subjunctive. It is not often found in modern English.

'What! is he not solid gold?' said the Swallow to himself. He was too polite to make any personal remarks out loud.

'Far away,' continued the statue in a low musical voice, 'far away in a little street there is a poor house. One of the windows is open, and through it I can see a woman seated at a table. Her face is thin and worn, and she has coarse, red hands, all pricked[1] by the needle, for she is a seamstress.[2] She is embroidering[3] passion-flowers on a satin gown for the loveliest of the Queen's maids-of-honour to wear at the next Court ball. In a bed in the corner of the room her little boy is lying ill. He has a fever, and is asking for oranges. His mother has nothing to give him but river water, so he is crying. Swallow, Swallow, little Swallow, will you not bring her the ruby out of my sword-hilt? My feet are fastened[4] to this pedestal and I cannot move.'

'I am waited for in Egypt,' said the Swallow. 'My friends are flying up and down the Nile, and talking to the large lotus-flowers. Soon they will go to sleep in the tomb of the great King. The King is there himself in his painted coffin. He is wrapped in yellow linen, and embalmed[5] with spices. Round his neck is a chain of pale green jade,[6] and his hands are like withered[7] leaves.'

'Swallow, Swallow, little Swallow,' said the Prince, 'will you not stay with me for one night, and be my

1. *pricked* : with very small holes made by needles.
2. *seamstress* ['siːmstrəs] : sewing-woman.
3. *embroidering* [ɪm'brɔɪdərɪŋ] : making designs on cloth by needlework.
4. *fastened* ['faːsnd] : attached, fixed.
5. *embalmed* [ɪm'baːmd] : preserved.
6. *jade* : hard, usually green stone, from which ornaments, etc. are made.
7. *withered* ['wɪðəd] : dry, dead.

messenger? The boy is so thirsty, and the mother so sad.'

'I don't think I like boys,' answered the Swallow. 'Last summer, when I was staying on the river, there were two rude boys, the miller's[1] sons, who were always throwing stones at me. They never hit me, of course; we swallows fly far too well for that, and besides I come of a family famous for its agility; but still, it was a mark of disrespect.'

But the Happy Prince looked so sad that the little Swallow was sorry. 'It is very cold here,' he said; 'but I will stay with you for one night, and be your messenger.'

'Thank you, little Swallow,' said the Prince.

So the Swallow picked out[2] the great ruby from the Prince's sword, and flew away with it in his beak over the roofs of the town.

He passed by the cathedral tower, where the white marble angels were sculptured. He passed by the palace and heard the sound of dancing. A beautiful girl came out on the balcony with her lover. 'How wonderful the stars are,' he said to her, 'and how wonderful is the power of love!'

'I hope my dress will be ready in time for the State-ball,'[3] she answered; 'I have ordered passion-flowers to be embroidered on it: but the seamstresses are so lazy.'

He passed over the river, and saw the lanterns hanging to the masts of the ships. He passed over the Ghetto, and saw the old Jews bargaining with each

1. *miller* : a person who grinds corn in a mill.
2. *picked out* : removed.
3. *State-ball* : an important ball or dance at which the head of state would be present.

other, and weighing out money in copper[1] scales.[2] At last he came to the poor house and looked in. The boy was tossing[3] feverishly on his bed, and the mother had fallen asleep, she was so tired. In he hopped, and laid the great ruby on the table beside the woman's thimble.[4] Then he flew gently round the bed, fanning[5] the boy's forehead with his wings. 'How cool I feel!' said the boy, 'I must be getting better'; and he sank into a delicious slumber.

Then the Swallow flew back to the Happy Prince, and told him what he had done. 'It is curious,' he remarked, 'but I feel quite warm now, although it is so cold.'

'That is because you have done a good action,' said the Prince. And the little Swallow began to think, and then he fell asleep. Thinking always made him sleepy.

When day broke he flew down to the river and had a bath. 'What a remarkable phenomenon!' said the Professor of Ornithology as he was passing over the bridge. 'A swallow in winter!' And he wrote a long letter about it to the local newspaper. Everyone quoted it, it was full of so many words that they could not understand.

'Tonight I go to Egypt,' said the Swallow, and he was in high spirits at the prospect. He visited all the public monuments, and sat a long time on the top of the church steeple.[6] Wherever he went the Sparrows chirruped, and said to each other, 'What a

1. *copper* : a reddish brown metal.
2. *scales* : instrument for weighing.
3. *tossing* : moving restlessly from side to side.
4. *thimble* : a small cap of metal (or plastic now) used to protect the finger and push the needle while sewing.
5. *fanning* : making a current of air as if with a fan.
6. *steeple* ['sti:pl] : a tall tower with a spire, rising from the roof of a church.

distinguished stranger!' so he enjoyed himself very much.

When the moon rose he flew back to the Happy Prince. 'Have you any commissions for Egypt?' he cried; 'I am just starting.'

'Swallow, Swallow, little Swallow,' said the Prince, 'will you not stay with me one night longer?'

'I am waited for in Egypt,' answered the Swallow. 'Tomorrow my friends will fly up to the Second Cataract. The river-horse couches[1] there among the bulrushes,[2] and on a great granite throne sits the God Memnon. All night long he watches the stars, and when the morning star shines he utters one cry of joy, and then he is silent. At noon the yellow lions come down to the water's edge to drink. They have eyes like green beryls,[3] and their roar is louder than the roar of the cataract.'

'Swallow, Swallow, little Swallow,' said the Prince, 'far away across the city I see a young man in a garret.[4] He is leaning over a desk covered with papers, and in a tumbler[5] by his side there is a bunch of withered violets. His hair is brown and crisp,[6] and his lips are red as a pomegranate, and he has large and dreamy eyes. He is trying to finish a play for the Director of the Theatre, but he is too cold to write any more. There is no fire in the grate,[7] and hunger has made him faint.'[8]

1. *couches* [kaʊtʃɪz] : lies.
2. *bulrushes* ['bʊlrʌʃɪz] : tall, thick water plants.
3. *beryls* : transparent precious stones, usually green.
4. *garret* : attic, poor room on the top floor of a house.
5. *tumbler* : a drinking glass.
6. *crisp* : "dry", in this context.
7. *grate* : metal frame holding coal.
8. *faint* : weak.

'I will wait with you one night longer,' said the Swallow, who really had a good heart. 'Shall I take him another ruby?'

'Alas! I have no ruby now,' said the Prince: 'my eyes are all that I have left. They are made of rare sapphires, which were brought out of India a thousand years ago. Pluck out[1] one of them and take it to him. He will sell it to the jeweller, and buy firewood, and finish his play.'

'Dear Prince,' said the Swallow, 'I cannot do that'; and he began to weep.

'Swallow, Swallow, little Swallow,' said the Prince, 'do as I command you.'

So the Swallow plucked out the Prince's eye, and flew away to the student's garret. It was easy enough to get in, as there was a hole in the roof. Through this he darted,[2] and came into the room. The young man had his head buried in his hands, so he did not hear the flutter of the bird's wings, and when he looked up he found the beautiful sapphire lying on the withered violets.

'I am beginning to be appreciated,' he cried; 'this is from some great admirer. Now I can finish my play,' and he looked quite happy.

The next day the Swallow flew down to the harbour. He sat on the mast of a large vessel and watched the sailors hauling big chests[3] out of the hold with ropes. 'Heave a-hoy!' they shouted as each chest came up. 'I am going to Egypt!' cried the Swallow, but nobody minded, and when the moon rose he flew back to the Happy Prince.

'I am come to bid you good-bye,'[4] he cried.

1. *Pluck out* : pull out.
2. *darted* : moved quickly.
3. *chests* : large boxes used to transport goods.
4. *bid you good-bye* : say goodbye (to you).

'Swallow, Swallow, little Swallow,' said the Prince, 'will you not stay with me one night longer?'

'It is winter,' answered the Swallow, 'and the chill snow will soon be here. In Egypt the sun is warm on the green palm-trees, and the crocodiles lie in the mud and look lazily about them. My companions are building a nest in the Temple of Baalbek, and the pink and white doves are watching them, and cooing[1] to each other. Dear Prince, I must leave you, but I will never forget you, and next spring I will bring you back two beautiful jewels in place of those you have given away. The ruby shall be redder than a red rose, and the sapphire shall be as blue as the great sea.'

'In the square below,' said the Happy Prince, 'there stands a little match-girl. She has let her matches fall in the gutter, and they are all spoiled. Her father will beat her if she does not bring home some money, and she is crying. She has no shoes or stockings, and her little head is bare. Pluck out my other eye, and give it to her, and her father will not beat her.'

'I will stay with you one night longer,' said the Swallow, 'but I cannot pluck out your eye. You would be quite blind then.'

'Swallow, Swallow, little Swallow,' said the Prince, 'do as I command you.'

So he plucked out the Prince's other eye, and darted down with it. He swooped past the match-girl, and slipped[2] the jewel into the palm of her hand. 'What a lovely bit of glass!' cried the little girl; and she ran home, laughing.

Then the Swallow came back to the Prince. 'You are blind now,' he said, 'so I will stay with you always.'

1. *cooing* : the noise made by doves.
2. *slipped* : placed gently (suggests an almost secretive action).

'No, little Swallow,' said the poor Prince, 'you must go away to Egypt.'

'I will stay with you always,' said the Swallow, and he slept at the Prince's feet.

All the next day he sat on the Prince's shoulder, and told him stories of what he had seen in strange lands. He told him of the red ibises,[1] who stand in long rows on the banks of the Nile, and catch goldfish in their beaks; of the Sphinx, who is as old as the world itself, and lives in the desert, and knows everything, of the merchants, who walk slowly by the side of their camels and carry amber beads in their hands; of the King of the Mountains of the Moon, who is as black as ebony, and worships a large crystal; of the great green snake that sleeps in a palm tree, and has twenty priests to feed it with honey-cakes; and of the pygmies who sail over a big lake on large flat leaves, and are always at war with the butterflies.

'Dear little Swallow,' said the Prince, 'you tell me of marvellous things, but more marvellous than anything is the suffering of men and of women. There is no Mystery so great as Misery. Fly over my city, little Swallow, and tell me what you see there.'

So the Swallow flew over the great city, and saw the rich making merry in their beautiful houses, while the beggars were sitting at the gates. He flew into dark lanes, and saw the white faces of starving children looking out listlessly[2] at the black streets. Under the archway of a bridge two little boys were lying in one another's arms to try and keep themselves warm. 'How hungry we are!' they said. 'You must not lie here,' shouted the watch-man, and they wandered out into the rain.

1. *ibises* : a wading bird like a heron.
2. *listlessly* : without vitality or enthusiasm.

Then he flew back and told the Prince what he had seen.

'I am covered with fine gold,' said the Prince, 'you must take it off, leaf by leaf, and give it to my poor; the living always think that gold can make them happy.'

Leaf after leaf of the fine gold the Swallow picked off, till the Happy Prince looked quite dull and grey. Leaf after leaf of the fine gold he brought to the poor, and the children's faces grew rosier,[1] and they laughed and played games in the street. 'We have bread now!' they cried.

Then the snow came, and after the snow came the frost. The streets looked as if they were made of silver, they were so bright and glistening;[2] long icicles like crystal daggers[3] hung down from the eaves[4] of the houses, everybody went about in furs, and the little boys wore scarlet caps and skated on the ice.

The poor little Swallow grew colder and colder, but he would not leave the Prince, he loved him too well. He picked up crumbs[5] outside the baker's door when the baker was not looking, and tried to keep himself warm by flapping[6] his wings.

But at last he knew that he was going to die. He had just enough strength to fly up to the Prince's shoulder once more. 'Good-bye, dear Prince!' he murmured, 'will you let me kiss your hand?'

1. *rosier* : pinker - more like the colour of a pink rose.
2. *glistening* : shining.
3. *daggers* : short, pointed, two-edged knifes used as a weapon.
4. *eaves* : the overhanging lower edges of a roof.
5. *crumbs* : very small pieces of bread or cake which have fallen off larger pieces.
6. *flapping* : making (his wings) move up and down quickly.

'I am glad that you are going to Egypt at last, little Swallow,' said the Prince, 'you have stayed too long here; but you must kiss me on the lips, for I love you.'

'It is not to Egypt that I am going,' said the Swallow. 'I am going to the House of Death. Death is the brother of Sleep, is he not?'

And he kissed the Happy Prince on the lips, and fell down dead at his feet.

At that moment a curious crack[1] sounded inside the statue, as if something had broken. The fact is that the leaden heart had snapped[2] right in two. It certainly was a dreadfully hard frost.

Early the next morning the Mayor was walking in the square below in company with the Town Councillors. As they passed the column he looked up at the statue: 'Dear me! how shabby the Happy Prince looks!' he said.

'How shabby, indeed!' cried the Town Councillors, who always agreed with the Mayor: and they went up to look at it.

'The ruby has fallen out of his sword, his eyes are gone, and he is golden no longer,' said the Mayor; 'in fact, he is little better than a beggar!'

'Little better than a beggar,' said the Town Councillors.

'And here is actually a dead bird at his feet!' continued the Mayor. 'We must really issue a proclamation that birds are not to be allowed to die here.' And the Town Clerk made a note of the suggestion.

So they pulled down the statue of the Happy Prince. 'As he is no longer beautiful he is no longer useful,' said the Art Professor at the University.

1. *crack* : sudden sharp noise.
2. *snapped* : broke suddenly with a sharp noise.

Then they melted[1] the statue in a furnace, and the Mayor held a meeting of the Corporation to decide what was to be done with the metal. 'We must have another statue, of course,' he said, 'and it shall be a statue of myself.'

'Of myself,' said each of the Town Councillors, and they, quarrelled. When I last heard of them they were quarrelling still.

'What a strange thing!' said the overseer[2] of the workmen at the foundry. 'This broken lead heart will not melt in the furnace. We must throw it away.' So they threw it on a dust-heap where the dead Swallow was also lying.

'Bring me the two most precious things in the city,' said God to one of His Angels; and the Angel brought Him the leaden heart and the dead bird.

'You have rightly chosen,' said God, 'for in my garden of Paradise this little bird shall sing for evermore, and in my city of gold the Happy Prince shall praise me.'

1. *melted* : reduced to liquid by heating.
2. *overseer* ['əʊvəsɪə$_r$] : a person whose job it is to see that work is properly done.

Pre-reading Activities

1. Think of some fairy stories or traditional tales in your language.
2. Have you noticed the importance of the number **three** in many traditional tales and fairy stories? There may be three sons or daughters, three suitors, three wishes, three days, three nights, three metals (gold, silver, lead), three animals. Did any of the stories you thought of make use of the number three? If not, think of examples of such stories now.
3. Make a list of stories in which animals, plants, or inanimate objects speak.
4. Think again about fables or fairy stories you know. Do they all have a moral? What is the moral of some of them?

Activities while Reading

Now read the first part of "The Happy Prince" up to "' ... Good-bye!' and he flew away" (p. 75).

1. Guess the meanings of the following words, then check them in your monolingual dictionary.

WORD	YOUR GUESS	DICTIONARY DEFINITION
muttered		
gazed		
slender		
courtship		
attachment		
twittered		

2. Describe the statue of the Happy Prince. Complete the grid.

POSITION OF THE STATUE	
COVERING OF THE BODY	
EYES	
SWORD-HILT	

3. Wilde, the narrator, allows the reader to see a number of different points of view in this passage. Complete the grid by saying what the following people think of the statue:

THE TOWN COUNCILLOR	
THE SENSIBLE MOTHER	
THE DISAPPOINTED MAN	
THE CHARITY CHILDREN	
THE MATHEMATICAL MASTER	

4. What contrast does Wilde make between the Charity Children and the Mathematical Master?

5. Describe the setting of the following:
   a. the opening of the story
   b. the Swallow's courtship of the Reed

6. At what time of year does the Swallow leave the Reed?

7. What words are used to describe the Swallow's courtship of the Reed in human terms?

8. Explain Wilde's play on words in the use of "attached" (p. 75).

9. What reasons does the Swallow give for leaving the Reed?

10. The Swallow comes to the city and lands between the feet of the Happy Prince. What do you think will be the relationship between the Swallow and the Happy Prince?

Now read from "All day long he flew..." (p. 75) to "Thinking always made him sleepy" (p. 80).

11. Guess the meanings of the following words, then check them in your monolingual dictionary.

Word	**Your Guess**	**Dictionary Definition**
drenched		
lofty		
fever		
coffin		
wrapped		
hopped		
slumber		

12. In the previous section, the sensible mother told her little boy that the Happy Prince never cried for anything. Why do we now see her words as ironical?

13. What contrast does the Happy Prince make between his feelings when he was alive and those now that he is dead?

14. Describe the seamstress and her child.

15. Describe the great Egyptian king.

16. What finally makes the little Swallow decide to take the great ruby to the seamstress?

17. The beautiful girl who comes on to the balcony of the royal palace says the seamstresses are so lazy. What irony does Wilde intend here?

18. What made the boy fall into "a delicious slumber"?

19. Why, according to the Happy Prince, is the little Swallow warm when he returns from the seamstress's?

Now read from "When day broke he flew down to the river..." (p. 80) to "... he looked quite happy" (p. 82).

20. Guess the meanings of the following words, then check them in your monolingual dictionary.

WORD	YOUR GUESS	DICTIONARY DEFINITION
chirruped utters pomegranate dreamy jeweller flutter		

21. When the Happy Prince asks the little Swallow to pluck out one of his eyes to take to the young writer, what is the reaction of the Swallow?

22. Describe the young man. Complete the grid.

Where does he live?	
What is he doing?	
What is on his desk?	
Physical characteristics:	
hair	
lips	
eyes	
Physical condition	

Now read from "The next day the Swallow flew down to the harbour." (p. 82) to "... and he slept at the Prince's feet" (p. 84).

23. Guess the meanings of the following words, then check them in your monolingual dictionary.

WORD	YOUR GUESS	DICTIONARY DEFINITION
harbour		
hauling		
chill		
spoiled		
swooped		

24. Describe the little match-girl, explaining why she is crying.

Try now to guess how the story will end, then read to the end.

25. What marvellous things did the little Swallow tell the Happy Prince about?

26. What does the little Swallow see when he flies over the city?

27. When the Happy Prince's heart snapped in two, Wilde writes: "It certainly was a dreadfully hard frost." Can you think of any other reason for the breaking of the Happy Prince's heart?

28. Describe the comments of the Town Councillors on the Happy Prince and the little Swallow. What contrast is there between their attitudes to the statue now and at the beginning of the story?

29. What does the quarrelling of the Town Councillors tell us about their characters?

30. Why are the leaden heart and the dead bird the two most precious things in the city?

Post-reading Activities

The Structure of the Story

The structure of "The Happy Prince" is that of many fairy stories and folk tales. (Refer to the points you considered in the Pre-reading Activities.) We know that Wilde was influenced by Hans Andersen and that he was writing with children in mind, though, as he said, the stories would appeal to anyone who retained something of the wonder and joy of childhood.
The story falls into the following parts:

a. Introduction (pp. 73-6).
b. The Happy Prince's story of his carefree life while he was alive contrasted with his present awareness of suffering.
c. The carrying out of the requests the Happy Prince makes to the little Swallow and the little Swallow's activities the day after he does his errands for the Happy Prince.
d. The contrast between the wonderful things the little Swallow tells the Happy Prince and the sufferings and injustice seen in the city.
e. The death of the Swallow, the broken heart of the Happy Prince and the subsequent destruction of his statue.
f. The "moral" of the tale.

We can distinguish between the **story** of a work of fiction and its **plot.** The story would be the events of the narrative seen chronologically and the plot would be the order in which they are treated in the narrative.
Does Wilde narrate everything in chronological order?
We can answer this question by looking first at the beginning of the story.
What is the first event?
We hear some Town Councillors talking about the statue of the Happy Prince, followed by comments by various other people.
When we are introduced to the little Swallow, we are told he flew over the city presumably at around the same time that the people

were talking about the Happy Prince, but then we are taken back in time to explain why the Swallow flew over the city at that particular time of the year. When his friends had flown to Egypt, he had stayed behind, having fallen in love with a Reed. Now, having fallen out of love with the Reed, he is on his way to Egypt to join his friends.
The little Swallow and the Happy Prince are brought together when the bird lands between the statue's feet.

1. Go through the rest of the story to check whether there are any further differences between **story** and **plot,** or whether from this point they coincide.

2. In the central part of the story, how many requests does the Happy Prince make of the little Swallow? In what way is the structure of the narrative here typical of fairy and folk tales?

3. In each of the narratives of the Prince's requests to the little Swallow, words are repeated. What are the repeated words, and what is the effect of the repetition?

4. At each of the three points when the Happy Prince asks the little Swallow to stay with him one more night, the little Swallow describes what his companions are doing in Egypt. Complete the following table, showing what the little Swallow says about his friends and Egypt.

FIRST DESCRIPTION	
SECOND DESCRIPTION	
THIRD DESCRIPTION	

5. Find a simile in each of the above three descriptions. What significance do these similes have in the structure of the narrative?

6. The day after each of the missions of the little Swallow, what does he do?

FIRST DAY	
SECOND DAY	
THIRD DAY	

How does this reinforce the tripartite structure of this central section of the narrative?

Themes

The themes of the story include love and friendship; the idea of sacrifice; riches and poverty; the contrast between physical and spiritual beauty. Which of these themes do you think most important and why? What other themes can you think of?
Keeping in mind the themes of the story, answer the following questions:

1. The result of the little Swallow's missions is that he decides to stay with the Happy Prince. Why?
2. What is the contrast between the sights seen by the little Swallow during his travels and those he sees on his flight over the city?
3. Describe how the Happy Prince loses his physical beauty and suggest how this reflects a growth in spiritual beauty.
4. Through his fable, what criticisms does Wilde make of his own society?
5. In what ways is your society like that of Wilde's fable?

Symbolism in "The Happy Prince"

What do the following symbolize in the story?

a. Egypt and the Nile;
b. the jewels and gold leaf on the statue of the Prince;
c. the breaking of the Prince's leaden heart.

General Questions

1. What ironical points does Wilde make when he brings back the Town Councillors towards the end of the story?

2. What is the moral of the story? Is it stated explicitly, or is it only implied by Wilde?

3. An "omniscient" narrator is a narrator who knows everything about his characters, even their inner thoughts. An omniscient narrator may be obtrusive, always telling the reader what to think, or unobtrusive, remaining in the background. How many direct authorial comments can you find in the story? On the whole, would you describe Wilde as an obtrusive or unobtrusive narrator?

Summarising

Complete the following summary of the story by filling the gaps. The infinitives of verbs required are given in brackets.

A swallow had fallen in love with a .... and, when his friends .... (migrate) to Egypt, he ....(remain) behind to court her. Becoming disillusioned with her, the swallow ....(decide) to join his friends in Egypt. On reaching a large city, the swallow stopped to rest and .... (choose) a place between the feet of a statue that .... (stand) on a high column. ....(feel) three drops of water falling on him, the swallow looked up and saw the eyes of the statue ....(fill) with tears. The statue .... (explain) to the swallow that when he ....(be) alive he .... (call) the Happy Prince. Now, however, that he ....(be) dead and set up high over the city he .... (be able to see) all the ugliness and .... of the city. Though the swallow wanted to continue on his .... to Egypt the Happy Prince asked his help in ....(relieve) some of the misery of the city. First the swallow ....(spend) a night taking a .... from the Happy Prince's sword-hilt to a poor woman with a .... child. The second night the swallow .... (take) one of the Happy Prince's eyes, which ....(make) of rare sapphires, to help a poor student. The third night the swallow ....(carry) the Happy Prince's other eye to help a poor little .... The swallow remained with the Happy Prince, instead of ....(fly) to Egypt. The Happy Prince asked him ....(fly) over the whole city and .... (report) everything that he saw. When the swallow returned, he .... (describe) what he ....(see). On ....(hear) of the poor children in the city, the Happy Prince asked the swallow .... (take off) all the gold leaf with which he ....(cover) and .... (give) it to the children. When the swallow ....(take) the gold leaf to the children, they

......................(become) very happy, because they .... (be able to buy) bread. But the poor swallow, in helping the Happy Prince, ... (delay) his journey to Egypt too long and, when winter came, ...(die) of cold. On the death of his friend, the swallow, the Happy Prince's heart .... (break) in two. When the Mayor and the Town .... passed .... and saw the statue ....(strip) of all its jewels and gold, they said how poor it looked, little better than a .... They also .... (note) the little swallow dead at the Prince's feet, which they ....(find) distasteful. It ....(decide) to pull .... the statue, but when some workmen ....(melt) it in a furnace, they found the heart ....(not melt) so they ....(throw) it on a dust heap where the swallow ....(also lie). God asked one of His Angels to bring him the two most .... things in the city and, to God's approval, the Angel ....(bring) Him the leaden heart and the dead bird. The bird ....(sing) in Paradise for evermore and the Happy Prince ....(praise) God.

The Nightingale and the Rose

'SHE SAID that she would dance with me if I brought her red roses,' cried the young Student, 'but in all my garden there is no red rose.'

From her nest in the holm-oak tree[1] the Nightingale heard him, and she looked out through the leaves and wondered.

'No red rose in all my garden!' he cried, and his beautiful eyes filled with tears. 'Ah, on what little things does happiness depend! I have read all that the wise men have written, and all the secrets of philosophy are mine, yet for want of a red rose is my life made wretched.'

'Here at last is a true lover,' said the Nightingale. 'Night after night have I sung of him though I knew him not:[2] night after night have I told[3] his story to the stars and now I see him. His hair is dark as the hyacinth-blossom, and his lips are red as the rose of his desire, but passion has made his face like pale ivory and sorrow has set her seal upon his brow.'

'The Prince gives a ball tomorrow night,' murmured the young Student, 'and my love will be of the

1. *holm-oak tree* : evergreen oak, with holly-like leaves (holly is used to decorate houses and churches at Christmas).
2. *knew him not* : this form of the negative is now archaic.
3. *have I told* : such inversions are now archaic.

company. If I bring her a red rose she will dance with me till dawn. If I bring her a red rose, I shall hold her in my arms, and she will lean her head upon my shoulder and her hand will be clasped[1] in mine. But there is no red rose in my garden, so I shall sit lonely and she will pass me by. She will have no heed of me,[2] and my heart will break.'

'Here, indeed, is the true lover,' said the Nightingale. 'What I sing of, he suffers: what is joy to me, to him is pain. Surely love is a wonderful thing. It is more precious than emeralds and dearer than fine opals. Pearls and pomegranates cannot buy it, nor is it set forth in the market-place. It may not be purchased of the merchants, nor can it be weighed out in the balance for gold.'

'The musicians will sit in their gallery,' said the young Student, 'and play upon their stringed instruments, and my love will dance to the sound of the harp and the violin. She will dance so lightly that her feet will not touch the floor, and the courtiers in their gay dresses will throng round her. But with me she will not dance, for I have no red rose to give her'; and he flung himself down[3] on the grass, and buried his face in his hands, and wept.

'Why is he weeping?' asked a little Green Lizard, as he ran past him with his tail in the air.

'Why, indeed?' said a Butterfly, who was fluttering[4] about after a sunbeam.

'Why, indeed?' whispered a Daisy to his neighbour, in a soft, low voice.

'He is weeping for a red rose,' said the Nightingale.

1. *clasped* : held tightly.
2. *have no heed of me* : pay no attention to me, ignore me.
3. *flung himself down* : threw himself down violently.
4. *fluttering* : flapping its wings and making short flights.

'For a red rose?' they cried; 'how very ridiculous!' and the little Lizard, who was something of a cynic, laughed outright.

But the Nightingale understood the secret of the Student's sorrow, and she sat silent in the oak-tree, and thought about the mystery of Love.

Suddenly she spread her brown wings for flight, and soared[1] into the air. She passed through the grove like a shadow and like a shadow she sailed across the garden.

In the centre of the grass-plot was standing a beautiful Rose-tree, and when she saw it she flew over to it, and lit[2] upon a spray.[3]

'Give me a red rose,' she cried, 'and I will sing you my sweetest song.'

But the Tree shook its head.

'My roses are white,' it answered; 'as white as the foam of the sea, and whiter than the snow on the mountain. But go to my brother who grows round the old sun-dial, and perhaps he will give you what you want.'

So the Nightingale flew over to the Rose-tree that was growing round the old sun-dial.

'Give me a red rose,' she cried, 'and I will sing you my sweetest song.'

But the Tree shook its head.

'My roses are yellow,' it answered; 'as yellow as the hair of the mermaiden[4] who sits upon an amber throne, and yellower than the daffodil that blooms in the meadow before the mower[5] comes with his

1. *soared* : flew high.
2. *lit* : landed.
3. *spray* : branch.
4. *mermaiden* : more often "mermaid" now: maid of the sea, half girl, half fish.
5. *mower* : one who cuts hay, corn, grass, etc.

scythe.[1] But go to my brother who grows beneath the Student's window, and perhaps he will give you what you want.'

So the Nightingale flew over to the Rose-tree that was growing beneath the Student's window.

'Give me a red rose,' she cried, 'and I will sing you my sweetest song.'

But the Tree shook its head.

'My roses are red,' it answered; 'as red as the feet of the dove, and redder than the great fans of coral that wave and wave in the ocean-cavern. But the winter has chilled my veins, and the frost has nipped my buds, and the storm has broken my branches, and I shall have no roses at all this year.'

'One red rose is all I want,' cried the Nightingale, 'only one red rose! Is there no way by which I can get it?'

'There is a way,' answered the Tree; 'but it is so terrible that I dare not tell it to you.'

'Tell it to me,' said the Nightingale, 'I am not afraid.'

'If you want a red rose,' said the Tree, 'you must build it out of music by moonlight, and stain it[2] with your own heart's-blood. You must sing to me with your breast against a thorn. All night long you must sing to me, and the thorn must pierce your heart, and your life-blood must flow into my veins, and become mine.'

'Death is a great price to pay for a red rose,' cried the Nightingale, 'and Life is very dear to all. It is pleasant to sit in the green wood, and to watch the Sun in his chariot of gold, and the Moon in her chariot

1. *scythe* [saɪð] : sharp instrument with curved blade for cutting hay, etc. The mower who comes with his scythe is a traditional symbol of death.
2. *stain it* : colour it.

of pearl. Sweet is the scent of the hawthorn,[1] and sweet are the bluebells[2] that hide in the valley, and the heather[3] that blows on the hill. Yet Love is better than Life, and what is the heart of a bird compared to the heart of a man?'

So she spread her brown wings for flight, and soared into the air. She swept over the garden like a shadow, and like a shadow she sailed through the grove.

The young Student was still lying on the grass, where she had left him, and the tears were not yet dry in his beautiful eyes.

'Be happy,' cried the Nightingale, 'be happy; you shall have your red rose. I will build it out of music by moonlight, and stain it with my own heart's-blood. All that I ask of you in return is that you will be a true lover, for Love is wiser than Philosophy, though he is wise, and mightier than Power, though he is mighty. Flame-coloured are his wings, and coloured like flame is his body. His lips are sweet as honey, and his breath is like frankincense.'

The Student looked up from the grass, and listened, but he could not understand what the Nightingale was saying to him, for he only knew the things that are written down in books.

But the Oak-tree understood, and felt sad, for he was very fond of the little Nightingale who had built her nest in his branches.

'Sing me one last song,' he whispered; 'I shall feel lonely when you are gone.'

1. *hawthorn* ['hɔːθɔːn] : a thorny shrub with white, red or pink blossom (flowers) and small dark red berries.
2. *bluebells* : blue flowers which have the shape of small bells.
3. *heather* : plant or shrub of the *erica* family.

So the Nightingale sang to the Oak-tree, and her voice was like water bubbling from a silver jar.

When she had finished her song, the Student got up, and pulled a note-book and a lead-pencil out of his pocket.

'She has form,' he said to himself, as he walked away through the grove—'that cannot be denied to her; but has she got feeling? I am afraid not. In fact, she is like most artists; she is all style, without any sincerity. She would not sacrifice herself for others. She thinks merely of music, and everybody knows that the arts are selfish. Still, it must be admitted that she has some beautiful notes in her voice. What a pity it is that they do not mean anything, or do any practical good!' And he went into his room, and lay down on his little pallet-bed,[1] and began to think of his love, and, after a time, he fell asleep.

And when the moon shone in the heavens the Nightingale flew to the Rose-tree, and set her breast against the thorn. All night long she sang, with her breast against the thorn, and the cold crystal Moon leaned down and listened. All night long she sang, and the thorn went deeper and deeper into her breast, and her life-blood ebbed away[2] from her.

She sang first of the birth of love in the heart of a boy and a girl. And on the topmost spray of the Rose-tree there blossomed[3] a marvellous rose, petal following petal, as song followed song. Pale was it, at first, as the mist that hangs over the river—pale as the feet of the morning, and silver as the wings of the dawn. As the shadow of a rose in a mirror of silver, as the shadow of a rose in a water-pool, so was the rose that blossomed on the topmost spray of the Tree.

1. *pallet-bed* : straw bed.
2. *ebbed away* : flowed away.
3. *blossomed* ['blɒsəmd] : flowered, bloomed.

But the Tree cried to the Nightingale to press closer against the thorn. 'Press closer, little Nightingale,' cried the Tree, 'or the Day will come before the rose is finished.'

So the Nightingale pressed closer against the thorn, and louder and louder grew her song, for she sang of the birth of passion in the soul of a man and a maid.

And a delicate flush [1] of pink came into the leaves of the rose, like the flush in the face of the bridegroom when he kisses the lips of the bride. But the thorn had not yet reached her heart, so the rose's heart remained white, for only a Nightingale's heart's-blood can crimson [2] the heart of a rose.

And the Tree cried to the Nightingale to press closer against the thorn. 'Press closer, little Nightingale,' cried the Tree, 'or the Day will come before the rose is finished.'

So the Nightingale pressed closer against the thorn, and the thorn touched her heart, and a fierce pang of pain shot through her. Bitter, bitter was the pain, and wilder and wilder grew her song, for she sang of the Love that is perfected by Death, of the Love that dies not in the tomb.

And the marvellous rose became crimson, like the rose of the eastern sky. Crimson was the girdle of petals,[3] and crimson as a ruby was the heart.

But the Nightingale's voice grew fainter,[4] and her little wings began to beat, and a film [5] came over her

1. *flush* : colour, tinge, shade.
2. *crimson* : make red. Later on this page Wilde uses "crimson" as an adjective: rich deep red.
3. *girdle of petals* : the petals that surrounded the heart of the rose.
4. *fainter* : weaker.
5. *film* : thin covering, like a mist, which prevented the dying nightingale from seeing clearly.

eyes. Fainter and fainter grew her song, and she felt something choking in her throat.

Then she gave one last burst of music. The white Moon heard it, and she forgot the dawn, and lingered on[1] in the sky. The red rose heard it, and it trembled all over with ecstasy, and opened its petals to the cold morning air. Echo bore it to her purple cavern in the hills, and woke the sleeping shepherds from their dreams. It floated through the reeds of the river, and they carried its message to the sea.

'Look, look!' cried the Tree, 'the rose is finished now'; but the Nightingale made no answer, for she was lying dead in the long grass, with the thorn in her heart.

And at noon the Student opened his window and looked out.

'Why, what a wonderful piece of luck!' he cried; 'here is a red rose! I have never seen any rose like it in all my life. It is so beautiful that I am sure it has a long Latin name'; and he leaned down and plucked it.

Then he put on his hat, and ran up to the Professor's house with the rose in his hand.

The daughter of the Professor was sitting in the doorway winding blue silk on a reel, and her little dog was lying at her feet.

'You said that you would dance with me if I brought you a red rose,' cried the Student. 'Here is the reddest rose in all the world. You will wear it tonight next[2] your heart, and as we dance together it will tell you how I love you.'

But the girl frowned.[3]

1. *lingered* ['lɪŋgəd] *on* : stayed as if not wanting to go.
2. *next* : modern English "next to".
3. *frowned* : wrinkled her forehead in disapproval.

'I am afraid it will not go with my dress,' she answered; 'and, besides, the Chamberlain's nephew has sent me some real jewels, and everybody knows that jewels cost far more than flowers.'

'Well, upon my word, you are very ungrateful,' said the Student angrily; and he threw the rose into the street, where it fell into the gutter,[1] and a cart-wheel went over it.

'Ungrateful!' said the girl. 'I tell you what, you are very rude; and, after all, who are you? Only a Student. Why, I don't believe you have even got silver buckles to your shoes as the Chamberlain's nephew has'; and she got up from her chair and went into the house.

'What a silly thing Love is!' said the Student as he walked away. 'It is not half as useful as Logic, for it does not prove anything, and it is always telling one of things that are not going to happen, and making one believe things that are not true. In fact, it is quite unpractical, and, as in this age to be practical is everything, I shall go back to Philosophy and study Metaphysics.'

So he returned to his room and pulled out a great dusty book, and began to read.

1. *gutter* : shallow channel at the side of the road to take water away to the drains.

Pre-reading Activities

1. What are nightingales usually associated with?
2. What do red roses usually symbolize?

Activities while Reading

1. Describe the opening scene ("She said that she would dance ... " to "... his beautiful eyes filled with tears.").
2. In all the Student's garden there is no red rose. What do you think is the symbolic meaning of this?
3.. The Student says all the secrets of philosophy are his but his life is made wretched "for want of a red rose". What contrast is Wilde suggesting here?
4. What in the student's appearance makes the Nightingale consider him a true lover?
5. "'Love is a wonderful thing'". How does the Nightingale suggest the wonder of love.
6. The Nightingale asks three rose-trees to give her a red rose. What are the responses of the three trees? Complete the grid.

	Responses
First Tree	
Second Tree	
Third Tree	

7. Guess the meanings of the following words on pages 107-8, then check them in your monolingual dictionary.

WORD	YOUR GUESS	DICTIONARY DEFINITION
chilled		
nipped		
pierce		
swept		

8. Each tree describes its roses with two similes. List the similes used by each tree.

	SIMILES
FIRST TREE	
SECOND TREE	
THIRD TREE	

Why does Wilde use these similes?

9. How does the Nightingale describe Love? Complete the grid.

DESCRIPTION OF LOVE	
WINGS	
BODY	
LIPS	
BREATH	

10. What is ironic about the description of the Student when he listens to the Nightingale's thoughts on Love?

11. The Oak-tree understands the Nightingale's song but the Student doesn't. What are the Student's reflections on the Nightingale's song?

12. Why does Wilde repeat "All night long" in the paragraph describing the Nightingale singing with its breast against the thorn?

13. Complete the grid to show the themes of the Nightingale's song and the phases of the growth of the red rose.

Theme of Song	**Phase of Growth of the Rose**

14. Describe the various reactions to the Nightingale's "one last burst of music".

	Reactions
The White Moon	
The Red Rose	
Echo	

15. On seeing the red rose, the Student says: "' It is so beautiful that I am sure it has a long Latin name'". What is Wilde ironically revealing about the student here?

16. Comment on the Professor's daughter's rejection of the Student. How does she show her snobbery and her superficiality?

17. When the Student rejects Love and turns to Philosophy and Metaphysics, he returns to his room and pulls out "a great dusty book". What is the symbolic significance of "dusty" here?

Post-reading Activities

Wilde's Language and Style

Repetition

In this type of folk tale the use of repetition is a frequent narrative device. In "The Nightingale and the Rose" we find use of repetition (with variation) from the beginning:
"' ... in all my garden there is no red rose'".
"' No red rose in all my garden'".
List at least three other uses of repetition in the story. Why do you think Wilde uses such repetitions?

Inversion

Examples: "Ah, on what little things **does** my life depend!"
"...for want of a red rose **is** my life made wretched."
(Note the position of the auxiliary verbs in bold.)
In modern English the first example would read: Ah, my life depends on such little things and the second: My life is made wretched.
List at least three other examples of inversion in the story.
Why does Wilde use such inversions?

Use of Similes

1. In Question 8 of the While-reading Activities you listed the similes used by the trees to describe their roses. Find other examples of the use of similes on pages 109-10.

2. Why does Wilde make use of such similes?

Structure of the Story

The first part of the story is structured by means of a series of speeches by the Student and the Nightingale's responses to each of these. In the Nightingale's responses we can note the use of similes to describe the Student's appearance and state of mind as a lover, and also to describe love itself. Following this opening juxtaposition of speeches, we have the questions and reactions of a little Green Lizard, a Butterfly and a Daisy. The Student has three main speeches, there are three reactions to his sorrow: in the world of fairy tale and folk tale, three is a number of special significance. What other use is made of sequences of three in the structure of the story?

Symbolism

What symbolic elements can you find in the story?

Presentation of the "Characters" of the Story

Which adjectives would be appropriate for the Student, the Professor's Daughter and the Nightingale.

frivolous	serious	sincere	insincere	shallow
profound	sensitive	insensitive	romantic	realistic
superficial	selfless	snobbish	intellectual	sentimental

STUDENT	PROFESSOR'S DAUGHTER	NIGHTINGALE

Themes

One important theme in the story is the contrast between warm love and cold philosophy. Wilde contrasts the love shown by the Nightingale with the Student's inability to understand anything outside his "dusty" books of philosophy. What other themes are important in the story? Make a comment on Wilde's treatment of each.

THEME	COMMENT

The Presence of Wilde in the Story

How far do we feel the presence of Wilde as a narrator? Look in the text for examples. (For consideration of narrative technique, see the Post-reading Activities on "The Canterville Ghost", pp. 67-68.)

The Selfish Giant

EVERY AFTERNOON, as they were coming from school, the children used to go and play in the Giant's garden.

It was a large lovely garden, with soft green grass. Here and there over the grass stood beautiful flowers like stars, and there were twelve peach-trees that in the spring-time broke out into delicate blossoms of pink and pearl, and in the autumn bore rich fruit. The birds sat on the trees and sang so sweetly that the children used to stop their games in order to listen to them. 'How happy we are here!' they cried to each other.

One day the Giant came back. He had been to visit his friend the Cornish ogre, and had stayed with him for seven years. After the seven years were over he had said all that he had to say, for his conversation was limited, and he determined to return to his own castle. When he arrived he saw the children playing in the garden.

'What are you doing here?' he cried in a very gruff voice, and the children ran away.

'My own garden is my own garden,' said the Giant; 'anyone can understand that, and I will allow nobody to play in it but myself.' So he built a high wall all round it, and put up a notice-board.

TRESPASSERS
WILL BE
PROSECUTED

He was a very selfish Giant.

The poor children had now nowhere to play. They tried to play on the road, but the road was very dusty and full of hard stones, and they did not like it. They used to wander round the high walls when their lessons were over, and talk about the beautiful garden inside. 'How happy we were there!' they said to each other.

Then the Spring came, and all over the country there were little blossoms and little birds. Only in the garden of the Selfish Giant it was still winter. The birds did not care to sing[1] in it as there were no children, and the trees forgot to blossom. Once a beautiful flower put its head out from the grass, but when it saw the notice-board it was so sorry for the children that it slipped back into the ground again, and went to sleep. The only people who were pleased were the Snow and the Frost. 'Spring has forgotten this garden,' they cried, 'so we will live here all the year round.' The Snow covered up the grass with her great white cloak, and the Frost painted all the trees silver. Then they invited the North Wind to stay with them, and he came. He was wrapped in furs, and he roared all day about the garden, and blew the chimney-pots down. 'This is a delightful spot,' he said, 'we must ask the Hail[2] on a visit.' So the Hail came. Every day for three hours he rattled[3] on the roof of the castle till he broke most of the slates, and then he ran round and round the garden as fast as he could go. He was dressed in grey, and his breath was like ice.

1. *did not care to sing* : did not want, had no desire to sing.
2. *Hail* : frozen rain falling in pellets or small pieces.
3. *rattled* : made a series of short, sharp sounds, quickly.

'I cannot understand why the Spring is so late in coming,' said the Selfish Giant, as he sat at the window and looked out at his cold, white garden, 'I hope there will be a change in the weather.'

But the Spring never came, nor the Summer. The Autumn gave golden fruit to every garden, but to the Giant's garden she gave none. 'He is too selfish,' she said. So it was always winter there, and the North Wind and the Hail, and the Frost, and the Snow danced about through the trees.

One morning the Giant was lying awake in bed when he heard some lovely music. It sounded so sweet to his ears that he thought it must be the King's musicians passing by. It was really only a little linnet[1] singing outside his window, but it was so long since he had heard a bird sing in his garden that it seemed to him to be the most beautiful music in the world. Then the Hail stopped dancing over his head, and the North Wind ceased roaring, and a delicious perfume came to him through the open casement. 'I believe the Spring has come at last,' said the Giant; and he jumped out of bed and looked out.

What did he see?

He saw a most wonderful sight. Through a little hole in the wall the children had crept in, and they were sitting in the branches of the trees. In every tree that he could see there was a little child. And the trees were so glad to have the children back again that they had covered themselves with blossoms, and were waving their arms gently above the children's heads. The birds were flying about and twittering[2] with delight, and the flowers were looking up through the

1. *linnet* : a common brown or grey bird known for its singing; a songbird.
2. *twittering* : chirping; making a succession of light tremulous sounds.

green grass and laughing. It was a lovely scene, only in one corner it was still winter. It was the farthest corner of the garden, and in it was standing a little boy. He was so small that he could not reach up to the branches of the tree, and he was wandering all round it, crying bitterly. The poor tree was still covered with frost and snow, and the North Wind was blowing and roaring above it. 'Climb up! little boy,' said the Tree, and it bent its branches down as low as it could; but the boy was too tiny.

And the Giant's heart melted[1] as he looked out. 'How selfish I have been!' he said: 'now I know why the Spring would not come here. I will put that poor little boy on the top of the tree, and then I will knock down the wall, and my garden shall be the children's playground for ever and ever.' He was really very sorry for what he had done.

So he crept downstairs and opened the front door quite softly, and went out into the garden. But when the children saw him they were so frightened that they all ran away, and the garden became winter again. Only the little boy did not run for his eyes were so full of tears that he did not see the Giant coming. And the Giant stole up behind him and took him gently in his hand, and put him up into the tree. And the tree broke at once into blossom, and the birds came and sang on it, and the little boy stretched out his two arms and flung[2] them round the Giant's neck, and kissed him. And the other children when they saw that the Giant was not wicked any longer, came running back, and with them came the Spring. 'It is your garden now, little children,' said the Giant, and he took a great axe and knocked down the wall. And when the people were going to market at twelve o'clock

1. *melted* : grew softer.
2. *flung* : threw (past tense of "to fling").

they found the Giant playing with the children in the most beautiful garden they had ever seen.

All day long they played, and in the evening they came to the Giant to bid him good-bye.

'But where is your little companion?' he said: 'the boy I put into the tree.' The Giant loved him the best because he had kissed him.

'We don't know,' answered the children: 'he has gone away.'

'You must tell him to be sure and come tomorrow,' said the Giant. But the children said that they did not know where he lived and had never seen him before; and the Giant felt very sad.

Every afternoon, when school was over, the children came and played with the Giant. But the little boy whom the Giant loved was never seen again. The Giant was very kind to all the children, yet he longed for[1] his first little friend, and often spoke of him. 'How I would like to see him!' he used to say.

Years went over,[2] and the Giant grew very old and feeble.[3] He could not play about any more, so he sat in a huge armchair, and watched the children at their games, and admired his garden. 'I have many beautiful flowers,' he said, 'but the children are the most beautiful flowers of all.'

One winter morning he looked out of his window as he was dressing. He did not hate the Winter now, for he knew that it was merely the Spring asleep, and that the flowers were resting.

Suddenly he rubbed his eyes in wonder and looked and looked. It certainly was a marvellous sight. In the farthest corner of the garden was a tree quite covered with lovely white blossoms. Its branches were golden,

1. *longed for* : desired strongly to see again.
2. *went over* : passed; modern English: "Years went by".
3. *feeble* : weak.

and silver fruit hung down from them, and underneath it stood the little boy he had loved.

Downstairs ran the Giant in great joy, and out into the garden. He hastened across the grass, and came near to the child. And when he came quite close his face grew red with anger, and he said, 'Who hath[1] dared to wound thee?'[2] For on the palms of the child's hands were the prints of two nails, and the prints of two nails were on the little feet.

'Who hath dared to wound thee?' cried the Giant, 'tell me, that I may take my big sword and slay him.'

'Nay,'[3] answered the child: 'but these are the wounds of Love.'

'Who art thou?'[4] said the Giant, and a strange awe fell on him, and he knelt before the little child. And the child smiled on[5] the Giant, and said to him, 'You let me play once in your garden, today you shall come with me to my garden, which is Paradise.'

And when the children ran in that afternoon, they found the Giant lying dead under the tree, all covered with white blossoms.

1. *hath* : archaic form of "has".
2. *thee* : archaic form of "you" (object form).
3. *Nay* (archaic) : No.
4. *Who art thou?* (archaic) : Who are you?
5. *smiled on* (archaic) : modern English: smiled at. All these archaic forms give a Biblical feel to the language.

Pre-reading Activity

In fairy or folk tales what is usually the role of the giant? Can you think of any unusual giants?

Activities while Reading

1. Guess the meanings of the following words, then check them in your monolingual dictionary.

WORD	YOUR GUESS	DICTIONARY DEFINITION
ogre		
gruff		
slipped		
wrapped		
spot		
slates		

2. What features of the Giant's garden are mentioned?

3. What joke does Wilde make in the third paragraph? What does this tell us about the Giant?

4. What two points show that the Giant was a very selfish one?

5. When Spring comes after the Giant's return to his garden, how have the features mentioned in Question 2 changed?

6. What four "people" inhabit the Giant's closed garden during Spring?

7. How was Spring brought back into the Giant's garden?

8. Why does one corner of the Giant's garden remain wintry?
9. How is the Giant converted from selfishness to love?
10. When the little boy that the Giant helped into the tree returns, what is his symbolic meaning?

Post-reading Activities

Wilde's Language and Style

1. The tale is told in quite simple language. Its different phases are shown in the changing descriptions of the flowers, the twelve peach-trees, the birds and the children. Follow the changes of description during the story.

IN THE GARDEN	CHANGE OF DESCRIPTION
The flowers	
The twelve peach-trees	
The birds	
The children	

2. At the end of the story, the Giant uses the old second person singular.

   a. Find examples of this. (Consult the notes.)
   b. Why does the Giant begin to use this form in addressing the child?

Symbolism

What examples of symbolism can you find in the story? Make a comment on each piece of symbolism that you find. (e.g. Is the use of the symbolism effective? What, if anything, does it add to the story?)

Themes

1. What do you think are the main themes of the tale?

2. What is the moral of the tale?

The presence of Wilde in the Story

Look at Question 3 of the While-reading Activities. Wilde gently intrudes into the story to make a passing joke. What other examples can you find of the presence of the narrator in the tale? To what extent is Wilde an obtrusive narrator in this story?

The Remarkable Rocket

THE KING'S SON was going to be married, so there were general rejoicings. He had waited a whole year for his bride, and at last she had arrived. She was a Russian Princess, and had driven all the way from Finland in a sledge drawn by six reindeer. The sledge was shaped like a great golden swan, and between the swan's wings lay the little Princess herself. Her long ermine[1] cloak reached right down to her feet, on her head was a tiny cap of silver tissue,[2] and she was as

1. *ermine* ['ɜːmɪn] : fur of the winter coat of a small carnivorous animal; white fur with black spots.
2. *silver tissue* : silver coloured cloth.

pale as the Snow Palace in which she had always lived. So pale was she that as she drove through the streets all the people wondered. 'She is like a white rose!' they cried, and they threw down flowers on her from the balconies.

At the gate of the Castle the Prince was waiting to receive her. He had dreamy violet eyes,[1] and his hair was like fine gold. When he saw her he sank upon[2] one knee, and kissed her hand.

'Your picture was beautiful,' he murmured, 'but you are more beautiful than your picture,' and the little Princess blushed.

'She was like a white rose before,' said a young Page to his neighbour, 'but she is like a red rose now'; and the whole Court was delighted.

For the next three days everybody went about saying, 'White rose, Red rose, Red rose, White rose' and the King gave orders that the Page's salary was to be doubled. As he received no salary at all this was not of much use to him, but it was considered a great honour, and was duly[3] published in the Court Gazette.

When the three days were over the marriage was celebrated. It was a magnificent ceremony, and the bride and bridegroom walked hand in hand under a canopy[4] of purple velvet embroidered[5] with little

1. *dreamy violet eyes* : violet-coloured eyes suggesting their owner was often in a reverie, thinking of beautiful unpractical things.
2. *sank upon* : went down on.
3. *duly* : rightly, properly.
4. *canopy* : covering.
5. *embroidered* : decorated with needlework; the little pearls were sewn on to the canopy.

pearls. Then there was a State Banquet, which lasted for five hours. The Prince and Princess sat at the top of the Great Hall and drank out of a cup of clear crystal. Only true lovers could drink out of this cup, for if false lips touched it, it grew grey and dull and cloudy.

'It is quite clear that they love each other,' said the little Page, 'as clear as crystal!' and the King doubled his salary a second time.

'What an honour!' cried all the courtiers.

After the banquet there was to be a Ball. The bride and bridegroom were to dance the Rose-dance together, and the King had promised to play the flute. He played very badly, but no one had ever dared to tell him so, because he was the King. Indeed, he knew only two airs, and was never quite certain which one he was playing; but it made no matter for, whatever he did, everybody cried out, 'Charming! charming!'

The last item on the programme was a grand display of fireworks, to be let off exactly at midnight. The little Princess had never seen a firework in her life, so the King had given orders that the Royal Pyrotechnist should be in attendance on the day of her marriage.

'What are fireworks like?' she had asked the Prince, one morning, as she was walking on the terrace.

'They are like the Aurora Borealis,' said the King, who always answered questions that were addressed to other people, 'only much more natural. I prefer them to stars myself, as you always know when they are going to appear, and they are as delightful as my own flute-playing. You must certainly see them.'

So at the end of the King's garden a great stand had been set up, and as soon as the Royal Pyrotechnist had put everything in its proper place, the fireworks began to talk to each other.

'The world is certainly very beautiful,' cried a little Squib.[1] 'Just look at those yellow tulips. Why! if they were real crackers[2] they could not be lovelier. I am very glad I have travelled. Travel improves the mind wonderfully, and does away with all one's prejudices.'

'The King's garden is not the world, you foolish Squib,' said a big Roman Candle; 'the world is an enormous place, and it would take you three days to see it thoroughly.'

'Any place you love is the world to you,' exclaimed the pensive Catharine Wheel,[3] who had been attached to an old deal[4] box in early life, and prided herself on her broken heart; 'but love is not fashionable any more, the poets have killed it. They wrote so much about it that nobody believed them, and I am not surprised. True love suffers, and is silent. I remember myself once – but no matter now. Romance is a thing of the past.'

'Nonsense!' said the Roman Candle. 'Romance never dies. It is like the moon, and lives for ever. The bride and bridegroom, for instance, love each other very dearly. I heard all about them this morning from a brown-paper cartridge,[5] who happened to be staying

1. *Squib* : small firework that burns with a hissing sound and then makes an explosion.
2. *crackers* : a "cracker" is another word for squib. The "crack" made by the cracker is the explosion.
3. *Catharine Wheel* (now spelt "Catherine") : a rotating firework, named after Saint Catherine, who was martyred on a spiked wheel.
4. *deal* : fir or pine wood.
5. *brown-paper cartridge* : a firework made of brown paper rolled into the form of a cartridge with gunpowder inside.

in the same drawer as myself, and he knew the latest Court news.'

But the Catharine Wheel shook her head. 'Romance is dead, Romance is dead, Romance is dead,' she murmured. She was one of those people who think that, if you say the same thing over and over a great many times, it becomes true in the end.

Suddenly, a sharp, dry cough was heard, and they all looked round.

It came from a tall, supercilious-looking Rocket, who was tied to the end of a long stick. He always coughed before he made any observations, so as to attract attention.

'Ahem! ahem!' he said, and everybody listened except the poor Catharine Wheel, who was still shaking her head, and murmuring, 'Romance is dead.'

'Order! order!' cried out a Cracker. He was something of a politician, and had always taken a prominent part in the local elections, so he knew the proper Parliamentary expressions to use.

'Quite dead,' whispered the Catharine Wheel, and she went off to sleep.

As soon as there was perfect silence, the Rocket coughed a third time and began. He spoke with a very slow, distinct voice, as if he were dictating his memoirs, and always looked over the shoulder of the person to whom he was talking. In fact, he had a most distinguished manner.

'How fortunate it is for the King's son,' he remarked, 'that he is to be married on the very day on which I am to be let off![1] Really, if it had not been arranged beforehand, it could not have turned out[2] better for him; but Princes are always lucky.'

1. *let off* : exploded.
2. *turned out* : happened.

'Dear me!' said the little Squib, 'I thought it was quite the other way, and that we were to be let off in the Prince's honour.'

'It may be so with you,' he answered; 'indeed, I have no doubt that it is, but with me it is different. I am a very remarkable Rocket, and come of remarkable parents. My mother was the most celebrated Catharine Wheel of her day, and was renowned for her graceful dancing. When she made her great public appearance she spun round nineteen times before she went out, and each time that she did so she threw into the air seven pink stars. She was three feet and a half in diameter, and made of the very best gunpowder. My father was a Rocket like myself, and of French extraction. He flew so high that the people were afraid that he would never come down again. He did, though, for he was of a kindly disposition, and he made a most brilliant descent in a shower of golden rain. The newspapers wrote about his performance in very flattering terms. Indeed, the Court Gazette called him a triumph of Pylotechnic art.'

'Pyrotechnic, Pyrotechnic, you mean,' said a Bengal Light;[1] 'I know it is Pyrotechnic, for I saw it written on my own canister.'[2]

'Well, I said Pylotechnic,' answered the Rocket, in a severe tone of voice, and the Bengal Light felt so crushed[3] that he began at once to bully the little squibs, in order to show that he was still a person of some importance.

'I was saying,' continued the Rocket, 'I was saying – What was I saying?'

1. *Bengal Light* : another type of firework.
2. *canister* ['kænɪstər] : small container, usually of metal.
3. *crushed* : put down, humiliated.

'You were talking about yourself,' replied the Roman Candle.

'Of course; I knew I was discussing some interesting subject when I was so rudely interrupted. I hate rudeness and bad manners of every kind, for I am extremely sensitive. No one in the whole world is so sensitive as I am, I am quite sure of that.'

'What is a sensitive person?' said the Cracker to the Roman Candle.

'A person who, because he has corns[1] himself, always treads on other people's toes,' answered the Roman Candle in a low whisper; and the Cracker nearly exploded with laughter.[2]

'Pray, what are you laughing at?' inquired the Rocket; 'I am not laughing.'

'I am laughing because I am happy,' replied the Cracker.

'That is a very selfish reason,' said the Rocket angrily. 'What right have you to be happy? You should be thinking about others. In fact, you should be thinking about me. I am always thinking about myself, and I expect everybody to do the same. That is what is called sympathy. It is a beautiful virtue, and I possess it in a high degree. Suppose, for instance, anything happened to me tonight, what a misfortune that would be for everyone! The Prince and Princess would never be happy again, their whole married life would be spoiled; and as for the King, I know he would not get over it.[3] Really, when I begin to reflect on the

1. *corns* : small, often painful, areas of hardened skin on the foot, especially on the toe.
2. *exploded with laughter* : there is a play on words. "To explode with laughter" is suddenly to begin to laugh loudly. Here there is also the literal meaning of "to explode".
3. *get over it* : recover from it.

importance of my position, I am almost moved to tears.'

'If you want to give pleasure to others,' cried the Roman Candle, 'you had better keep yourself dry.'

'Certainly,' exclaimed the Bengal Light, who was now in better spirits; 'that is only common sense.'

'Common sense, indeed!' said the Rocket indignantly; 'you forget that I am very uncommon, and very remarkable. Why, anybody can have common sense, provided that they have no imagination. But I have imagination, for I never think of things as they really are; I always think of them as being quite different. As for keeping myself dry, there is evidently no one here who can at all appreciate an emotional nature. Fortunately for myself, I don't care. The only thing that sustains one through life is the consciousness of the immense inferiority of everybody else, and this is a feeling I have always cultivated. But none of you have any hearts. Here you are laughing and making merry just as if the Prince and Princess had not just been married.'

'Well, really,' exclaimed a small Fire-balloon,[1] 'why not? It is a most joyful occasion, and when I soar up[2] into the air I intend to tell the stars all about it. You will see them twinkle[3] when I talk to them about the pretty bride.'

'Ah! what a trivial[4] view of life!' said the Rocket; 'but it is only what I expected. There is nothing in

1. *Fire-balloon* : a balloon made buoyant by the heat of the fire burning at its mouth.
2. *soar up* : fly high.
3. *twinkle* : shine with rapid intermittent gleams of light.
4. *trivial* : superficial.

you; you are hollow and empty. Why, perhaps the Prince and Princess may go to live in a country where there is a deep river, and perhaps they may have one only son, a little fair-haired boy with violet eyes like the Prince himself; and perhaps some day he may go out to walk with his nurse; and perhaps the nurse may go to sleep under a great elder-tree; [1] and perhaps the little boy may fall into the deep river and be drowned. What a terrible misfortune! Poor people, to lose their only son! It is really too dreadful! I shall never get over it.'

'But they have not lost their only son,' said the Roman Candle; 'no misfortune has happened to them at all.'

'I never said that they had,' replied the Rocket; 'I said that they might. If they had lost their only son there would be no use in saying any more about the matter. I hate people who cry over spilt milk.[2] But when I think that they might lose their only son, I certainly am very much affected.'[3]

'You certainly are!' cried the Bengal Light. 'In fact, you are the most affected person I ever met.'

'You are the rudest person I ever met,' said the Rocket, 'and you cannot understand my friendship for the Prince.'

'Why, you don't even know him,' growled the Roman Candle.

'I never said I knew him,' answered the Rocket. 'I dare say[4] that if I knew him I should not be his friend at all. It is a very dangerous thing to know one's friends.'

1. *elder-tree* : low white-flowered, dark-fruited tree.
2. *cry over spilt milk* : cry about something that has happened and cannot be changed.
3. *affected* : full of affectation, artificial.
4. *I dare say* : it is very probable.

'You had really better keep yourself dry,' said the Fire-balloon. 'That is the important thing.'

'Very important for you, I have no doubt,' answered the Rocket, 'but I shall weep if I choose'; and he actually burst into real tears, which flowed down his stick like rain-drops, and nearly drowned two little beetles, who were just thinking of setting up house together, and were looking for a nice dry spot to live in.

'He must have a truly romantic nature,' said the Catharine Wheel, 'for he weeps when there is nothing at all to weep about'; and she heaved a deep sigh [1] and thought about the deal box.

But the Roman Candle and the Bengal Light were quite indignant, and kept saying, 'Humbug![2] humbug!' at the top of their voices.[3] They were extremely practical, and whenever they objected to anything they called it humbug.

Then the moon rose like a wonderful silver shield; and the stars began to shine, and a sound of music came from the palace.

The Prince and Princess were leading the dance. They danced so beautifully that the tall white lilies [4] peeped in at the window and watched them, and the great red poppies [5] nodded their heads and beat time.

Then ten o'clock struck, and then eleven, and then twelve, and at the last stroke of midnight everyone came out on the terrace, and the King sent for the Royal Pyrotechnist.

1. *heaved a deep sigh* : sighed profoundly.
2. *Humbug!* : Rubbish! Used to condemn something as false or sham.
3. *at the top of their voices* : very loudly.
4. *lilies* (sing. lily) : a type of flower.
5. *poppies* (sing. poppy) : red flowers, with narcotic properties.

'Let the fireworks begin,' said the King; and the Royal Pyrotechnist made a low bow, and marched down to the end of the garden. He had six attendants with him, each of whom carried a lighted torch at the end of a long pole.

It was certainly a magnificent display.

Whizz! Whizz![1] went the Catharine Wheel, as she spun round and round. Boom! Boom! went the Roman Candle. Then the Squibs danced all over the place, and the Bengal Lights made everything look scarlet. 'Good-bye,' cried the Fire-balloon, as he soared away, dropping tiny blue sparks. Bang! Bang! answered the Crackers, who were enjoying themselves immensely. Every one was a great success except the Remarkable Rocket. He was so damped with crying that he could not go off at all. The best thing in him was the gunpowder, and that was so wet with tears that it was of no use. All his poor relations, to whom he would never speak, except with a sneer, shot up into the sky like wonderful golden flowers with blossoms of fire. Huzza! Huzza! cried the Court; and the little Princess laughed with pleasure.

'I suppose they are reserving me for some grand occasion,' said the Rocket; 'no doubt that is what it means,' and he looked more supercilious than ever.

The next day the workmen came to put everything tidy. 'This is evidently a deputation,' said the Rocket; 'I will receive them with becoming dignity'; so he put his nose in the air, and began to frown severely, as if he were thinking about some very important subject. But they took no notice of him at all till they were just going away. Then one of them caught sight of him.

1. *Whizz! Whizz!* : represents the sound of something moving quickly through the air (onomatopœia).

'Hallo!' he cried, 'what a bad rocket!' and he threw him over the wall into the ditch.

'BAD Rocket? BAD Rocket?' he said, as he whirled through the air; 'impossible! GRAND Rocket, that is what the man said. BAD and GRAND sound very much the same, indeed they often are the same'; and he fell into the mud.

'It is not comfortable here,' he remarked, 'but no doubt it is some fashionable watering-place, and they have sent me away to recruit[1] my health. My nerves are certainly very much shattered,[2] and require rest.'

Then a little Frog, with bright jewelled eyes, and a green mottled[3] coat, swam up to him.

'A new arrival, I see!' said the Frog. 'Well, after all there is nothing like mud. Give me rainy weather and a ditch and I am quite happy. Do you think it will be a wet afternoon? I am sure I hope so, but the sky is quite blue and cloudless. What a pity!'

'Ahem! ahem!' said the Rocket, and he began to cough.

'What a delightful voice you have!' cried the Frog. 'Really it is quite like a croak,[4] and croaking is, of course, the most musical sound in the world. You will hear our glee-club[5] this evening. We sit in the old duck-pond close by the farmer's house, and as soon as the moon rises we begin. It is so entrancing[6] that everybody lies awake to listen to us. In fact, it was only yesterday that I heard the farmer's wife say to

1. *recruit* : recover (archaic in this sense).
2. *shattered* : destroyed.
3. *mottled* : with spots.
4. *croak* : the sound made by a frog.
5. *glee-club* : club devoted to choral singing.
6. *entrancing* : delightful.

her mother that she could not get a wink of sleep[1] at night on account of us. It is most gratifying to find oneself so popular.'

'Ahem! ahem!' said the Rocket angrily. He was very much annoyed that he could not get a word in.

'A delightful voice, certainly,' continued the Frog, 'I hope you will come over to the duck-pond. I am off to look for my daughters. I have six beautiful daughters, and I am so afraid the Pike[2] may meet them. He is a perfect monster, and would have no hesitation in breakfasting off them. Well, good-bye; I have enjoyed our conversation very much, I assure you.'

'Conversation, indeed!' said the Rocket. 'You have talked the whole time yourself. That is not conversation.'

'Somebody must listen,' answered the Frog, 'and I like to do all the talking myself. It saves time, and prevents arguments.'

'But I like arguments,' said the Rocket.

'I hope not,' said the Frog complacently. 'Arguments are extremely vulgar, for everybody in good society holds exactly the same opinions. Good-bye a second time; I see my daughters in the distance'; and the little Frog swam away.

'You are a very irritating person,' said the Rocket, 'and very ill-bred.[3] I hate people who talk about themselves, as you do, when one wants to talk about oneself, as I do. It is what I call selfishness, and selfishness is a most detestable thing, especially to anyone of my temperament, for I am well known for

1. *wink of sleep* : a moment's sleep.
2. *Pike* : large voracious freshwater fish.
3. *ill-bred* : badly brought up.

my sympathetic nature. In fact, you should take example by me; you could not possibly have a better model. Now that you have the chance you had better avail yourself of it,[1] for I am going back to Court almost immediately. I am a great favourite at Court; in fact, the Prince and Princess were married yesterday in my honour. Of course, you know nothing of these matters, for you are a provincial.'

'There is no good talking to him,' said a Dragon-fly,[2] who was sitting on the top of a large brown bulrush;[3] 'no good at all, for he has gone away.'

'Well, that is his loss, not mine,' answered the Rocket. 'I am not going to stop talking to him merely because he pays no attention. I like hearing myself talk. It is one of my greatest pleasures. I often have long conversations all by myself, and I am so clever that sometimes I don't understand a single word of what I am saying.'

'Then you should certainly lecture on Philosophy,' said the Dragon-fly, and he spread a pair of lovely gauze[4] wings and soared away into the sky.

'How very silly of him not to stay here!' said the Rocket. 'I am sure that he has not often got such a chance of improving his mind. However, I don't care a bit. Genius like mine is sure to be appreciated some day'; and he sank down a little deeper into the mud.

After some time a large White Duck swam up to him. She had yellow legs, and webbed feet,[5] and

1. *avail yourself of it* : make use of it.
2. *Dragon-fly* : insect with long slender body and two pairs of wings.
3. *bulrush* : a water plant.
4. *gauze* [gɔːz]: thin transparent fabric of silk, cotton, etc.
5. *webbed* [webd] *feet* : with membranes filling the spaces between the toes, as with ducks' feet.

was considered a great beauty on account of her waddle.[1]

'Quack, quack, quack,' she said. 'What a curious shape you are! May I ask were you born like that, or is it the result of an accident?'

'It is quite evident that you have always lived in the country,' answered the Rocket, 'otherwise you would know who I am. However, I excuse your ignorance. It would be unfair to expect other people to be as remarkable as oneself. You will no doubt be surprised to hear that I can fly up into the sky, and come down in a shower of golden rain.'

'I don't think much of that,' said the Duck, 'as I cannot see what use it is to anyone. Now, if you could plough[2] the fields like the ox,[3] or draw[4] a cart like the horse, or look after the sheep like the collie-dog,[5] that would be something.'

'My good creature,' cried the Rocket in a very haughty tone of voice, 'I see that you belong to the lower orders. A person of my position is never useful. We have certain accomplishments,[6] and that is more than sufficient. I have no sympathy myself with industry of any kind, least of all with such industries as you seem to recommend. Indeed, I have always been of the opinion that hard work is simply the refuge of people who have nothing whatever to do.'

'Well, well,' said the Duck, who was of a very peaceful disposition, and never quarrelled with anyone,

1. *waddle* ['wɒdl] : characteristic way of walking of ducks, geese, etc.
2. *plough* : turn over (the earth).
3. *ox* : any bovine animal.
4. *draw* : pull.
5. *collie-dog* : sheepdog originating from Scotland.
6. *accomplishments* : skills, especially social.

'everybody has different tastes. I hope, at any rate, that you are going to take up your residence here.'

'Oh! dear no,' cried the Rocket. 'I am merely a visitor, a distinguished visitor. The fact is that I find this place rather tedious. There is neither society here, nor solitude. In fact, it is essentially suburban. I shall probably go back to Court, for I know that I am destined to make a sensation in the world.'

'I had thoughts of entering public life once myself,' remarked the Duck; 'there are so many things that need reforming. Indeed, I took the chair[1] at a meeting some time ago, and we passed resolutions condemning everything that we did not like. However, they did not seem to have much effect. Now I go in for domesticity, and look after my family.'

'I am made for public life,' said the Rocket, 'and so are all my relations, even the humblest of them. Whenever we appear we excite great attention. I have not actually appeared myself, but when I do so it will be a magnificent sight. As for domesticity, it ages one rapidly, and distracts one's mind from higher things.'

'Ah! the higher things of life, how fine they are!' said the Duck; 'and that reminds me how hungry I feel'; and she swam away down the stream, saying, 'Quack, quack, quack.'

'Come back! come back!' screamed the Rocket, 'I have a great deal to say to you'; but the Duck paid no attention to him. 'I am glad that she has gone', he said to himself, 'she has a decidedly middle-class mind', and he sank a little deeper still into the mud, and began to think about the loneliness of genius, when suddenly two

1. *took the chair*: acted as chairman.

little boys in white smocks[1] came running down the bank with a kettle and some faggots.[2]

'This must be the deputation,' said the Rocket, and he tried to look very dignified.

'Hallo!' cried one of the boys, 'look at this old stick; I wonder how it came here;' and he picked the rocket out of the ditch.

"OLD Stick!" said the Rocket, "impossible! GOLD Stick, that is what he said. Gold Stick is very complimentary. In fact, he mistakes me for one of the Court dignitaries!'[3]

'Let us put it into the fire!' said the other boy, 'it will help to boil the kettle.'

So they piled[4] the faggots together, and put the Rocket on top, and lit the fire.

'This is magnificent,' cried the Rocket, 'they are going to let me off in broad daylight,[5] so that everyone can see me.'

'We will go to sleep now', they said, 'and when we wake up the kettle will be boiled': and they lay down on the grass, and shut their eyes.

The Rocket was very damp, so he took a long time to burn. At last, however, the fire caught him.

'Now I am going off!' he cried, and he made himself very stiff and straight. 'I know I shall go much higher than the stars, much higher than the moon, much higher than the sun. In fact, I shall go so high that—'

Fizz! Fizz! Fizz! and he went straight up into the air.

'Delightful!' he cried, 'I shall go on like this for ever. What a success I am!'

1. *smocks* : a smock is a type of overall to keep clothes clean.
2. *faggots* : pieces of wood for burning.
3. *Court dignitaries* : officials of the court.
4. *piled* : made into a heap.
5. *in broad daylight* : in full daylight.

But nobody saw him.

Then he began to feel a curious tingling[1] sensation all over him.

'Now I am going to explode,' he cried. 'I shall set the whole world on fire, and make such a noise that nobody will talk about anything else for a whole year.' And he certainly did explode. Bang! Bang! Bang! went the gunpowder. There was no doubt about it.

But nobody heard him, not even the two little boys, for they were sound asleep.[2]

Then all that was left of him was the stick, and this fell down on the back of a Goose who was taking a walk by the side of the ditch.

'Good heavens!' cried the Goose. 'It is going to rain sticks'; and she rushed into the water.

'I knew I should create a great sensation,' gasped the Rocket, and he went out.

1. *tingling* : throbbing, stinging.
2. *sound asleep* : completely asleep; in a deep sleep.

Pre-reading Activities

1. How many fireworks can you think of?
2. What are fireworks used to celebrate in your country?

Activities while Reading

The story can be divided into six sections of unequal length.

Section A

Read from the beginning of the story to "the fireworks began to talk to each other" (p. 141).

1. Guess the meanings of the following words, then check them in your monolingual dictionary.

Word	Your Guess	Dictionary Definition
sledge		
blushed		
airs		
Pyrotechnist		
stand		

2. How does Wilde's description make the Prince and Princess seem like figures from a fairy-tale?
3. What is amusing about the King's twice doubling the young Page's salary?

Section B

Read from '"The world is certainly very beautiful"' (p. 141) to "They were extremely practical, and whenever they objected to anything they called it humbug" (p. 148).

1. Wilde was a famous playwright, and most of this passage is in the form of dialogue. How does Wilde characterise the different fireworks in their dialogue and in narrative comments?

Firework	Impression Given by the Characters When They Speak	Wilde's Comments
the little Squib		
the Roman Candle		
the Catharine Wheel		
the Rocket		
the Bengal Light		
the Fire-balloon		

2. Thinking of your answer to Question 1, list the character traits of the Rocket that Wilde ridicules.

Section C

Read from "Then the moon rose" (p. 148) to "... and he looked more supercilious than ever" (p. 149).

1. How does Wilde suggest the beauty of the dancing of the Prince and Princess?

2. In what two ways does Wilde describe the firework display?

3. How does Wilde suggest the Rocket's lack of self-knowledge in this section?

Section D

Read from "The next day the workmen came" (p. 149) to "he sank a little deeper into the mud" (p. 152).

How does the Rocket continue to deceive himself in this section? Complete the grid.

After the visit of the workmen	
While he is lying in the mud of the ditch	
During his conversation with the frog	
In his comments to the dragon-fly after the frog has gone away	

Section E

Read from "After some time a large White Duck" (p. 152) to '"Quack, quack, quack"' (p. 154).

1. What is ridiculous in the comment on the White Duck's beauty?

2. How does the Rocket try to assert his superiority over the Duck?

3. What does the White Duck seem to think of "public life" (p. 154)?

4. What is the Rocket's opinion of domesticity?

SECTION F

Read from '"Come back! come back!"' (p. 154) to the end of the story.

How does the Rocket further show his self-deception in the episode with the two little boys?

Post-reading Activities

1. There is a great deal of satire in this story. How does Wilde mock the King in Section A of the story?

2. In the second section, as well as mocking the Rocket (see Section B, Q. 1), Wilde satirises various human types in his treatment of the fireworks. Complete the grid, suggesting what Wilde mocks through his description of each of the fireworks.

FIREWORK	**OBJECT OF SATIRE**
the little Squib (p. 141)	
the Catharine Wheel (pp. 141-42)	
the Bengal Light (p. 143)	
the Roman Candle and the Bengal Light (p. 148)	

3. In what way does Wilde satirise the upper classes in Section E?

Characterisation

1. Referring to your answers to questions in the While-reading Activities, write a character-sketch of the Remarkable Rocket, showing his decline and fall.
2. Write brief character-sketches of any TWO minor characters.

The Presence of Wilde in the Story

Wilde's presence is often felt in what seem to be almost humorous asides. For example, when the King doubles the Page's salary, Wilde comments: "As he received no salary at all this was not of much use to him, but it was considered a great honour, and was duly published in the Court Gazette." Find other examples of amusing authorial comments.

Themes

Study the list of themes below and try to put them in their order of importance in the story. Give reasons for your decisions.

- **a.** Vanity.
- **b.** Illusion and reality.
- **c.** Snobbery and social climbing in high society.
- **d.** Common sense versus imagination. (See pp. 144-5.)
- **e.** Affectation versus sincerity.

The Birthday of the Infanta

IT WAS the birthday of the Infanta.[1] She was just twelve years of age, and the sun was shining brightly in the gardens of the palace.

Although she was a real Princess and the Infanta of Spain, she had only one birthday every year, just like the children of quite poor people, so it was naturally a matter of great importance to the whole country that she should have a really fine day for the occasion. And a really fine day it certainly was. The tall striped tulips stood straight up upon their stalks, like long rows of soldiers, and looked defiantly across the grass at the roses, and said: 'We are quite as splendid as you are now.' The purple butterflies fluttered about[2] with gold dust on their wings, visiting each flower in turn; the little lizards crept out of the crevices of the wall, and lay basking[3] in the white glare;[4] and the pomegranates split and cracked with the heat, and showed their bleeding red hearts. Even the pale yellow lemons, that hung in such profusion from the

1. *Infanta* : daughter of the King and Queen of Spain.
2. *fluttered about* : flew around.
3. *basking* : enjoying the sun and light.
4. *glare* : fierce brilliant light.

mouldering[1] trellis[2] and along the dim arcades,[3] seemed to have caught a richer colour from the wonderful sunlight, and the magnolia trees opened their great globe-like blossoms[4] of folded ivory, and filled the air with a sweet heavy perfume.

The little Princess herself walked up and down the terrace with her companions, and played hide and seek round the stone vases and the old moss-grown[5] statues. On ordinary days she was only allowed to play with children of her own rank, so she had always to play alone, but her birthday was an exception, and the King had given orders that she was to invite any of her young friends whom she liked to come and amuse themselves with her. There was a stately grace about these slim Spanish children as they glided about,[6] the boys with their large-plumed hats and short fluttering cloaks, the girls holding up the trains of their long brocade gowns, and shielding the sun from their eyes with huge fans[7] of black and silver. But the Infanta was the most graceful of all, and the most tastefully attired,[8] after the somewhat cumbrous[9] fashion of the day. Her robe was of grey satin, the skirt and the wide puffed sleeves[10] heavily embroidered[11] with silver, and

1. *mouldering* ['məʊldərɪŋ] : crumbling to dust.
2. *trellis* : structure to support climbing plants.
3. *arcades* : covered walks.
4. *blossoms* [blɒsəmz] : flowers.
5. *moss-grown* : overgrown with moss, a *herbaceous* plant, which grows, for example, on stones, walls, etc.
6. *glided about* : moved about gracefully.
7. *fans* : folding devices for cooling one's face.
8. *attired* : dressed.
9. *cumbrous* : heavy, difficult to move in.
10. *puffed sleeves* : sleeves drawn in at the wrist but left full.
11. *embroidered* : ornamented or decorated with needlework.

the stiff corset studded with[1] rows of fine pearls. Two tiny slippers with big pink rosettes peeped out beneath her dress as she walked. Pink and pearl was her great gauze fan, and in her hair, which like an aureole of faded gold stood out stiffly round her pale little face, she had a beautiful white rose.

From a window in the palace the sad melancholy King watched them. Behind him stood his brother, Don Pedro of Aragon, whom he hated, and his confessor, the Grand Inquisitor of Granada, sat by his side. Sadder even than usual was the King, for as he looked at the Infanta bowing with childish gravity to the assembling courtiers, or laughing behind the fan at the grim Duchess of Albuquerque who always accompanied her, he thought of the young Queen, her mother, who but a short time before – so it seemed to him – had come from the gay country of France, and had withered away[2] in the sombre splendour of the Spanish court, dying just six months after the birth of her child, and before she had seen the almonds blossom twice in the orchard, or plucked[3] the second year's fruit from the old gnarled[4] fig-tree that stood in the centre of the now grass-grown courtyard. So great had been his love for her that he had not suffered even the grave to hide her from him. She had been embalmed[5] by a Moorish physician, who in return for this service had been granted his life, which for heresy and suspicion of magical practices had been already forfeited,[6] men said, to the Holy Office,[7] and

1. *studded with* : decorated with.
2. *withered away* : declined in health until she died.
3. *plucked* : picked.
4. *gnarled* : twisted, with protuberances.
5. *embalmed* : preserved from decay with spices.
6. *forfeited* ['fɔːfɪtɪd] : made subject to the penalty of death.
7. *the Holy Office* : the Inquisition.

her body was still lying on its tapestried bier[1] in the black marble chapel of the Palace just as the monks had borne[2] her on that windy March day nearly twelve years before. Once every month the King, wrapped in[3] a dark cloak and with a muffled lantern[4] in his hand, went in and knelt by her side calling out, *'Mi reina! Mi reina!'* and sometimes breaking through the formal etiquette that in Spain governs every separate action of life, and sets limits even to the sorrow of a King, he would clutch at[5] the pale jewelled hands in a wild agony of grief, and try to wake by his mad kisses the cold painted[6] face.

Today he seemed to see her again, as he had seen her first at the Castle of Fontainebleau, when he was but fifteen years of age, and she still younger. They had been formally betrothed[7] on that occasion by the Papal Nuncio in the presence of the French King and all the Court, and he had returned to the Escurial[8] bearing with him a little ringlet[9] of yellow hair, and the memory of two childish lips bending down to kiss his hand as he stepped into his carriage. Later on had followed the marriage, hastily performed at Burgos, a small town on the frontier between the two countries, and the grand public entry into Madrid with the customary celebration of high mass at the Church of

1. *bier* : frame on which a dead body or coffin is placed. The bier is covered with tapestry.
2. *borne* : carried.
3. *wrapped in* : dressed in, covered by.
4. *muffled lantern* : lantern with the intensity of its light reduced. "Muffled" is usually used for sound.
5. *clutch at* : take hold of and hold tightly.
6. *painted* : coloured, made up to look as if she were alive.
7. *betrothed* : formally promised to each other in marriage.
8. *Escurial* : large royal palace and monastery built during the reign of Philip II (1527-98).
9. *ringlet* : curl (small ring).

La Atocha, and a more than usually solemn *auto-da-fé*,[1] in which nearly three hundred heretics, among whom were many Englishmen, had been delivered over to the secular arm to be burned.

Certainly he had loved her madly, and to the ruin, many thought, of his country, then at war with England for the possession of the empire of the New World. He had hardly ever permitted her to be out of his sight; for her, he had forgotten, or seemed to have forgotten, all grave affairs of State; and, with that terrible blindness that passion brings upon its servants, he had failed to notice that the elaborate ceremonies by which he sought to please her did but aggravate the strange malady from which she suffered. When she died he was, for a time, like one bereft[2] of reason. Indeed, there is no doubt but that he would have formally abdicated and retired to the great Trappist[3] monastery at Granada, of which he was already titular Prior, had he not been afraid to leave the little Infanta at the mercy of his brother, whose cruelty, even in Spain, was notorious, and who was suspected by many of having caused the Queen's death by means of a pair of poisoned gloves that he had presented to her on the occasion of her visiting his castle in Aragon. Even after the expiration of the three years of public mourning that he had ordained throughout his whole dominions by royal edict, he would never suffer his ministers to speak about any new alliance,[4] and when the Emperor himself sent to

1. *auto-da-fè* : literally, act of faith; the ceremony at which heretics were burnt after being condemned by the Inquisition.
2. *bereft* : deprived.
3. *Trappist* : member of a branch of the Cistercian Order, founded in 1664 at La Trappe and noted for silence and austerity.
4. *alliance* : marriage.

him, and offered him the hand of the lovely Archduchess of Bohemia, his niece, in marriage, he bade[1] the ambassadors tell their master that the King of Spain was already wedded to Sorrow, and that though she was but a barren[2] bride he loved her better than Beauty; an answer that cost his crown the rich provinces of the Netherlands, which soon after, at the Emperor's instigation, revolted against him under the leadership of some fanatics of the Reformed Church.

His whole married life, with its fierce, fiery-coloured[3] joys and the terrible agony of its sudden ending, seemed to come back to him today as he watched the Infanta playing on the terrace. She had all the Queen's pretty petulance of manner, the same wilful way of tossing her head,[4] the same proud, curved, beautiful mouth, the same wonderful smile – *vrai sourire de France*[5] indeed – as she glanced up now and then at the window, or stretched out her little hand for the stately Spanish gentlemen to kiss. But the shrill[6] laughter of the children grated on[7] his ears, and the bright pitiless sunlight mocked[8] his sorrow, and a dull odour of strange spices, such as embalmers use, seemed to taint[9] – or was it fancy? – the clear morning air. He buried his face in his hands, and when the Infanta looked up again the curtains had been drawn, and the King had retired.

1. *bade* : ordered.
2. *barren* : infertile.
3. *fiery-coloured* : red is the colour of passion.
4. *tossing her head* : throwing back her head (in contempt or impatience).
5. *vrai sourire de France* : real smile of France.
6. *shrill* : high-pitched.
7. *grated on* : had an irritating effect on.
8. *mocked* : ridiculed, made fun of.
9. *taint* : infect.

She made a little *moue*[1] of disappointment, and shrugged her shoulders.[2] Surely he might have stayed with her on her birthday. What did the stupid State affairs matter? Or had he gone to that gloomy[3] chapel, where the candles were always burning, and where she was never allowed to enter? How silly of him, when the sun was shining so brightly, and everybody was so happy! Besides, he would miss the sham[4] bull-fight for which the trumpet was already sounding, to say nothing of the puppet[5] show and the other wonderful things. Her uncle and the Grand Inquisitor were much more sensible. They had come out on the terrace, and paid her nice compliments. So she tossed her pretty head, and taking Don Pedro by the hand, she walked slowly down the steps towards a long pavilion of purple silk that had been erected at the end of the garden, the other children following in strict order of precedence, those who had the longest names going first.

A procession of noble boys, fantastically dressed[6] as *toreadors*, came out to meet her, and the young Count of Tierra-Nueva, a wonderfully handsome lad of about fourteen years of age, uncovering his head with all the grace of a born hidalgo and grandee[7] of

1. *moue* : pout - a pushing forward of the lips in disappointment, frustration, etc.
2. *shrugged her shoulders* : lifted and let fall her shoulders in annoyance.
3. *gloomy* : dark and depressing.
4. *sham* : pretended, not real.
5. *puppet* ['pʌpɪt] : marionette.
6. *fantastically dressed* : fancifully, extravagantly dressed.
7. *hidalgo and grandee* : a hidalgo is a lower ranking nobleman while a grandee is a higher ranking nobleman.
   There is a contradiction here, but Wilde evidently liked the sound of hidalgo and was not worried about accuracy.

Spain, led her solemnly in to a little gilt and ivory chair that was placed on a raised daïs[1] above the arena. The children grouped themselves all round, fluttering their big fans and whispering to each other, and Don Pedro and the Grand Inquisitor stood laughing at the entrance. Even the Duchess – the Camerera-Mayor[2] as she was called – a thin, hard-featured[3] woman with a yellow ruff,[4] did not look quite so bad-tempered as usual, and something like a chill[5] smile flitted across her wrinkled face and twitched[6] her thin bloodless lips.

It certainly was a marvellous bull-fight, and much nicer, the Infanta thought, than the real bull-fight that she had been brought to see at Seville, on the occasion of the visit of the Duke of Parma to her father. Some of the boys pranced about[7] on richly-caparisoned[8] hobby-horses,[9] brandishing[10] long javelins with gay streamers[11] of bright ribands[12] attached to them; others went on foot, waving their scarlet cloaks before

1. *daïs* ['deɪɪs]: low platform.
2. *Camerera-Mayor* [meə$_r$]: chief Lady of the Bedchamber, Lady-in-Waiting to a queen or princess. The Camerera would also be responsible for the Infanta's education.
3. *hard-featured* [ˌhaːd'fiːtʃəd] : having ugly features (facial characteristics).
4. *ruff* : frill of white linen or cotton worn round the neck.
5. *chill* : cold.
6. *twitched* : caused to move slightly.
7. *pranced about* : moved like horses with little jumps.
8. *richly-caparisoned* [rɪtʃli kə'pærɪsnd] : richly decorated.
9. *hobby-horses* : toy horses, made of wicker-work (basket-work).
10. *brandishing* : waving about.
11. *streamers* : pennons, long narrow flags, ribbons.
12. *ribands* : ribbons.

the bull, and vaulting lightly over[1] the barrier when he charged them; and as for the bull himself, he was just like a live bull, though he was only made of wickerwork and stretched hide,[2] and sometimes insisted on running round the arena on his hind legs, which no live bull ever dreams of doing. He made a splendid fight of it too, and the children got so excited that they stood up upon the benches, and waved their lace handkerchiefs and cried out: *Bravo toro! Bravo toro!* just as sensibly as if they had been grown-up people. At last, however, after a prolonged combat, during which several of the hobby-horses were gored through and through,[3] and their riders dismounted, the young Count of Tierra-Nueva brought the bull to his knees, and having obtained permission from the Infanta to give the *coup de grâce*,[4] he plunged his wooden sword into the neck of the animal with such violence that the head came right off, and disclosed the laughing face of little Monsieur de Lorraine, the son of the French Ambassador at Madrid.

The arena was then cleared amidst much applause, and the dead hobby-horses dragged solemnly away by two Moorish pages[5] in yellow and black liveries,[6] and after a short interlude, during which a French posture-master performed upon a tight-rope, some Italian puppets appeared in the semi-classical tragedy

1. *vaulting ... over* : jumping over something, using one hand as a support.
2. *hide* : leather.
3. *gored through and through* : pierced completely through by the bull's horns.
4. *coup-de-grâce* [ˌku:dəˈgra:s] : finishing stroke (the death blow).
5. *pages* : boys employed to attend on a person of high rank.
6. *liveries* (sing. livery): uniform worn by a servant.

of *Sophonisba* on the stage of a small theatre that had been built up for the purpose. They acted so well, and their gestures were so extremely natural, that at the close of the play the eyes of the Infanta were quite dim with tears. Indeed some of the children really cried, and had to be comforted with sweetmeats,[1] and the Grand Inquisitor himself was so affected that he could not help saying to Don Pedro that it seemed to him intolerable that things made simply out of wood and coloured wax, and worked mechanically by wires, should be so unhappy and meet with such terrible misfortunes.

An African juggler[2] followed, who brought in a large flat basket covered with a red cloth, and having placed it in the centre of the arena, he took from his turban a curious reed pipe,[3] and blew through it. In a few moments the cloth began to move, and as the pipe grew shriller and shriller two green and gold snakes put out their strange wedge-shaped[4] heads and rose slowly up, swaying to and fro[5] with the music as a plant sways in the water. The children, however, were rather frightened at their spotted hoods[6] and quick darting[7] tongues, and were much more pleased when the juggler made a tiny orange-tree grow out of the sand and bear pretty white blossoms and clusters[8]

1. *sweetmeats* : sweets.
2. *juggler* : one who performs feats of dexterity by throwing up and catching balls, clubs, etc.
3. *reed pipe* : musical instrument in the form of a pipe made from a reed.
4. *wedge-shaped* : in the form of a wedge, a piece of wood or metal forming an acute angle at one end.
5. *swaying to and fro* : moving the body one way and then the other.
6. *hoods* : a hood is a covering for the head and neck. Here it refers to the hood-like shape of the snakes' heads.
7. *darting* : quickly moving in and out.
8. *clusters* : bunches, fruit growing together in groups.

of real fruit; and when he took the fan of the little daughter of the Marquess de Las-Torres, and changed it into a blue bird that flew all round the pavilion and sang, their delight and amazement knew no bounds.[1] The solemn minuet, too, performed by the dancing boys from the church of Nuestra Señora Del Pilar, was charming. The Infanta had never before seen this wonderful ceremony which takes place every year at Maytime in front of the high altar of the Virgin, and in her honour; and indeed none of the royal family of Spain had entered the great cathedral of Saragossa since a mad priest, supposed by many to have been in the pay of Elizabeth of England, had tried to administer a poisoned wafer[2] to the Prince of the Asturias.[3] So she had known only by hearsay[4] of 'Our Lady's Dance', as it was called, and it certainly was a beautiful sight. The boys wore old-fashioned court dresses of white velvet, and their curious three cornered hats were fringed with[5] silver and surmounted with huge plumes of ostrich feathers, the dazzling whiteness of their costumes, as they moved about in the sunlight, being still more accentuated by their swarthy[6] faces and long black hair. Everybody was fascinated by the grave dignity with which they moved through the intricate figures of the dance, and by the elaborate grace of their slow gestures, and stately bows, and when they had finished their performance and doffed[7] their great plumed hats to

1. *bounds* : limits.
2. *wafer* : thin piece of type of bread used in the communion service.
3. *Prince of the Asturias* : the Crown Prince of Spain, the heir to the throne.
4. *by hearsay* : by being told.
5. *fringed with* : having an ornamental border of.
6. *swarthy* : dark.
7. *doffed* : took off (their hats) as a mark of respect.

the Infanta, she acknowledged their reverence with much courtesy, and made a vow that she would send a large wax candle to the shrine of Our Lady of Pilar in return for the pleasure that she had given her.

A troop of handsome Egyptians – as the gipsies were termed in those days – then advanced into the arena, and sitting down cross-legged, in a circle, began to play softly upon their zithers,[1] moving their bodies to the tune, and humming, almost below their breath, a low dreamy air. When they caught sight of Don Pedro they scowled[2] at him, and some of them looked terrified, for only a few weeks before he had two of their tribe hanged for sorcery[3] in the market-place at Seville, but the pretty Infanta charmed them as she leaned back peeping[4] over her fan with her great blue eyes, and they felt sure that one so lovely as she was could never be cruel to anybody. So they played on very gently and just touched the cords of the zithers with their long pointed nails, and their heads began to nod as though they were falling asleep. Suddenly, with a cry so shrill that all the children were startled, and Don Pedro's hand clutched[5] at the agate[6] pommel[7] of his dagger,[8] they leapt to their feet and whirled madly round the enclosure beating their tambourines, and chanting some wild love-song in their strange guttural language. Then at another signal, they all

1. *zithers* : stringed instruments.
2. *scowled* : looked sullenly or in a hostile way.
3. *sorcery* : witchcraft.
4. *peeping* : looking. It was only just possible to see her eyes as she looked.
5. *clutched* : held tightly.
6. *agate* ['ægət] : a type of quartz; a semi-precious stone.
7. *pommel* ['pɒml] : knob, especially at the end of a sword-hilt.
8. *dagger* : a type of knife; a stabbing weapon.

flung[1] themselves again to the ground and lay there quite still, the dull strumming[2] of the zithers being the only sound that broke the silence. After that they had done this several times, they disappeared for a moment and came back leading a brown shaggy[3] bear by a chain, and carrying on their shoulders some little Barbary apes.[4] The bear stood upon his head with the utmost gravity, and the wizened[5] apes played all kinds of amusing tricks with two gipsy boys who seemed to be their masters, and fought with tiny swords, and fired off guns, and went through the regular soldier's drill[6] just like the King's own bodyguard. In fact the gipsies were a great success.

But the funniest part of the whole morning's entertainment, was undoubtedly the dancing of the little Dwarf. When he stumbled[7] into the area, waddling[8] on his crooked[9] legs and wagging[10] his huge misshapen[11] head from side to side, the children went off into a loud shout of delight, and the Infanta herself laughed so much that the Camerera was obliged to remind her that although there were many precedents in Spain for a King's daughter weeping before her equals, there were none for a Princess of the blood

1. *flung* : threw.
2. *strumming* : sound made by plucking the strings of a guitar, etc., here the zither.
3. *shaggy* : with a long and rough coat.
4. *Barbary apes* : apes from Barbary, the old name for the western part of North Africa.
5. *wizened* : dried up, shrivelled (of the skins of the apes).
6. *drill* : set of exercises, here military exercises.
7. *stumbled* : walked almost falling.
8. *waddling* ['wɒdlɪŋ] : walking like a duck.
9. *crooked* ['krʊkɪd]: bent, not straight.
10. *wagging* : moving his head from side to side.
11. *misshapen* [ˌmɪs'ʃeɪpən] : badly shaped.

royal making so merry before those who were her inferiors in birth. The Dwarf, however, was really quite irresistible, and even at the Spanish Court, always noted for its cultivated passion for the horrible, so fantastic a little monster had never been seen. It was his first appearance, too. He had been discovered only the day before, running wild through the forest, by two of the nobles who happened to have been hunting in a remote part of the great cork-wood [1] that surrounded the town, and had been carried off by them to the Palace as a surprise for the Infanta; his father, who was a poor charcoal-burner,[2] being but too well pleased to get rid of so ugly and useless a child. Perhaps the most amusing thing about him was his complete unconsciousness of his own grotesque appearance. Indeed he seemed quite happy and full of the highest spirits. When the children laughed, he laughed as freely and as joyously as any of them, and at the close of each dance he made them each the funniest of bows,[3] smiling and nodding at them just as if he was really one of themselves, and not a little misshapen thing that Nature, in some humourous [4] mood, had fashioned for others to mock at. As for the Infanta, she absolutely fascinated him. He could not keep his eyes off her, and seemed to dance for her alone, and when at the close of the performance, remembering how she had seen the great ladies of the Court throw bouquets to Caffarelli, the famous Italian treble,[5] whom the Pope had sent from his own chapel

1. *cork-wood* : wood where trees are grown for their bark, which is cork.
2. *charcoal-burner* : a workman who burns wood to provide charcoal.
3. *bows* [baʊz] : bendings of the body, for example to receive applause, as here.
4. *humourous* : now spelt "humorous".
5. *treble* : singer with high voice, here presumably a *castrato*.

to Madrid that he might cure the King's melancholy by the sweetness of his voice, she took out of her hair the beautiful white rose, and, partly for a jest and partly to tease[1] the Camerera, threw it to him across the arena with her sweetest smile, he took the whole matter quite seriously, and pressing the flower to his rough coarse lips he put his hand upon his heart, and sank on one knee before her, grinning from ear to ear, and with his bright eyes sparkling[2] with pleasure.

This so upset the gravity of the Infanta that she kept on laughing long after the little Dwarf had run out of the arena, and expressed a desire to her uncle that the dance should be immediately repeated. The Camerera, however, on the plea that the sun was too hot, decided that it would be better that her Highness should return without delay to the Palace, where a wonderful feast had been already prepared for her, including a real birthday cake with her own initials worked all over it in painted sugar and a lovely silver flag waving from the top. The Infanta accordingly[3] rose up with much dignity, and having given orders that the little Dwarf was to dance again for her after the hour of siesta, and conveyed[4] her thanks to the young Count of Tierra-Nueva for his charming reception, she went back to her apartments, the children following in the same order in which they had entered.

Now when the little Dwarf heard that he was to dance a second time before the Infanta, and by her own express command, he was so proud that he ran out into the garden, kissing the white rose in an

1. *tease* : annoy in a playful way.
2. *sparkling* : shining brightly.
3. *accordingly* : therefore.
4. *conveyed* : communicated, expressed.

absurd ecstasy of pleasure, and making the most uncouth [1] and clumsy gestures of delight.

The Flowers were quite indignant at his daring to intrude into their beautiful home, and when they saw him capering [2] up and down the walks, and waving his arms above his head in such a ridiculous manner, they could not restrain their feelings any longer.

'He is really far too ugly to be allowed to play in any place where we are,' cried the Tulips.

'He should drink poppy-juice,[3] and go to sleep for a thousand years,' said the great scarlet Lilies, and they grew quite hot and angry.

'He is a perfect horror!' screamed the Cactus. 'Why, he is twisted and stumpy,[4] and his head is completely out of proportion with his legs. Really he makes me feel prickly [5] all over, and if he comes near me I will sting him with my thorns.'

'And he has actually got one of my best blooms,'[6] exclaimed the white Rose-tree. 'I gave it to the Infanta this morning myself, as a birthday present, and he has stolen it from her.' And she called out: 'Thief, thief, thief!' at the top of her voice.

Even the red Geraniums, who did not usually give themselves airs, and were known to have a great many poor relations themselves, curled up in disgust when they saw him, and when the Violets meekly remarked that though he was certainly extremely plain,[7] still he could not help it, they retorted with a good deal of

1. *uncouth* [ʌn'kuːθ] : awkward.
2. *capering* ['keɪpərɪŋ] : moving in a lively way.
3. *poppy-juice* : the poppy has narcotic qualities.
4. *stumpy* : short, like a stump.
5. *prickly* : a play on words: a) having prickles like a cactus; b) tingling.
6. *blooms* : flowers.
7. *plain* : the opposite of good-looking; here "ugly".

justice that was his chief defect, and that there was no reason why one should admire a person because he was incurable; and indeed, some of the Violets themselves felt that the ugliness of the little Dwarf was almost ostentatious, and that he would have shown much better taste if he had looked sad, or at least pensive, instead of jumping about merrily, and throwing himself into such grotesque and silly attitudes.

As for the old Sundial,[1] who was an extremely remarkable individual, and had told the time of day to no less a person than the Emperor Charles V himself, he was so taken aback[2] by the little Dwarf's appearance, that he almost forgot to mark two whole minutes with his long shadowy finger, and could not help saying to the great milk-white Peacock, who was sunning herself on the balustrade,[3] that everyone knew that the children of Kings were Kings, and that the children of charcoal-burners were charcoal-burners, and that it was absurd to pretend that it wasn't so; a statement with which the Peacock entirely agreed, and indeed screamed out, 'Certainly, certainly,' in such a loud, harsh[4] voice that the Gold-fish who lived in the basin of the cool splashing fountain put their heads out of the water, and asked the huge stone Tritons[5] what on earth was the matter.

1. *Sundial* : an instrument showing the time by the shadows cast by the sun.
2. *taken aback* : surprised, disconcerted.
3. *balustrade* : low wall at the edge of a balcony; parapet.
4. *harsh* : rough, unpleasant.
5. *Tritons* : imaginary semi-human sea-monsters. This paragraph contains allusions (the milk-white peacock, the goldfish) to Tennyson's poem "Now sleeps the crimson petal, now the white.

But somehow the Birds liked him. They had seen him often in the forest, dancing about like an elf[1] after the eddying[2] leaves, or crouched up[3] in the hollow of some old oak-tree, sharing his nuts with the squirrels. They did not mind his being ugly a bit. Why, even the Nightingale herself, who sang so sweetly in the orange groves at night that sometimes the Moon leaned down to listen, was not much to look at after all, and, besides, he had been kind to them, and during that terribly bitter winter when there were no berries on the trees, and the ground was as hard as iron, and the wolves had come down to the very gates of the city to look for food, he had never once forgotten them, but had always given them crumbs out of his little hunch[4] of black bread, and divided with them whatever poor breakfast he had.

So they flew round and round him, just touching his cheek with their wings as they passed, and chattered to each other, and the little Dwarf was so pleased that he could not help showing them the beautiful white rose, and telling them that the Infanta herself had given it to him because she loved him.

They did not understand a single word of what he was saying, but that made no matter, for they put their heads on one side, and looked wise, which is quite as good as understanding a thing, and very much easier.

The Lizards also took an immense fancy to him, and when he grew tired of running about and flung himself down on the grass to rest, they played and romped all over him, and tried to amuse him in the best way they could. 'Everyone cannot be as beautiful

1. *elf* : little supernatural creature.
2. *eddying* : moving around in circles; swirling.
3. *crouched up* : sitting with legs bent close up to the body.
4. *hunch* : thick piece.

as a lizard,' they cried; 'that would be too much to expect. And, though it sounds absurd to say so, he is really not so ugly after all, provided, of course, that one shuts one's eyes, and does not look at him.' The Lizards were extremely philosophical by nature, and often sat thinking for hours and hours together, when there was nothing else to do, or when the weather was too rainy for them to go out.

The Flowers, however, were excessively annoyed at their behaviour, and at the behaviour of the Birds. 'It only shows,' they said, 'what a vulgarizing effect this incessant rushing and flying about has. Well-bred[1] people always stay in exactly the same place, as we do. No one ever saw us hopping[2] up and down the walks, or galloping madly through the grass after dragon-flies. When we want a change of air, we send for the gardener, and he carries us to another bed. This is dignified, and as it should be. But birds and lizards have no sense of repose, and indeed birds have not even a permanent address. They are vagrants like the gipsies, and should be treated in exactly the same manner.' So they put their noses in the air, and looked very haughty,[3] and were quite delighted when after some time they saw the little Dwarf scramble up[4] from the grass, and make his way across the terrace to the palace.

'He should certainly be kept indoors for the rest of his natural life,' they said. 'Look at his hunched[5] back, and his crooked legs,' and they began to titter.[6]

1. *Well-bred* : having good breeding or manners.
2. *hopping* : jumping (on one leg).
3. *haughty* : arrogant.
4. *scramble up* : get to his feet quickly.
5. *hunched* : with a hunch or hump.
6. *titter* : laugh in a suppressed way.

But the little Dwarf knew nothing of all this. He liked the birds and lizards immensely, and thought that the flowers were the most marvellous things in the whole world, except of course the Infanta, but then she had given him the beautiful white rose, and she loved him, and that made a great difference. How he wished that he had gone back with her! She would have put him on her right hand, and smiled at him, and he would have never left her side, but would have made her his playmate, and taught her all kinds of delightful tricks. For though he had never been in a palace before, he knew a great many wonderful things. He could make little cages out of rushes for the grasshoppers [1] to sing in, and fashion the long-jointed bamboo [2] into the pipe that Pan [3] loves to hear. He knew the cry of every bird, and he could call the starlings from the tree-top, or the heron from the mere.[4] He knew the trail [5] of every animal, and could track [6] the hare by its delicate footprints, and the boar [7] by the trampled [8] leaves. All the wild dances he knew, the mad dance in red raiment [9] with the autumn, the light dance in blue sandals over the corn, the dance with the white snow-wreaths [10] in winter, and the

1. *grasshoppers* : jumping and chirping insects.
2. *long-jointed bamboo* : the bamboo has long pieces between its joints.
3. *Pan* : god of Nature.
4. *mere* : lake.
5. *trail* : marks made by the footprints of animals.
6. *track* : follow by observing signs, especially footprints.
7. *boar* : male wild pig.
8. *trampled* : walked upon and so beaten down.
9. *raiment* : clothes. Wilde is referring to the movement of the fallen red leaves.
10. *snow-wreaths* ['snəʊriːðz]: the wind blows the snow into the shape of wreathes, circular forms.

blossom-dance,[1] through the orchards[2] in spring. He knew where the wood-pigeons built their nests, and once when the fowler[3] had snared[4] the parent birds, he had brought up the young ones himself, and had built a little dovecot[5] for them in the cleft[6] of a pollard elm.[7] They were quite tame, and used to feed out of his hands every morning. She would like them, and the rabbits that scurried about[8] in the long fern, and the jays with their steely feathers and black bills,[9] and the hedgehogs that could curl themselves up into prickly balls, and the great wise tortoises that crawled slowly about, shaking their heads and nibbling at[10] the young leaves. Yes, she must certainly come to the forest and play with him. He would give her his own little bed, and would watch outside the window till dawn, to see that the wild, horned cattle[11] did not harm[12] her, nor the gaunt[13] wolves creep too near the hut. And at dawn he would tap at the shutters[14] and wake her, and they would go out and dance together all the day long. It was really not a bit lonely in the forest. Sometimes a Bishop rode through on his white

1. *blossom-dance* : dance of flowers.
2. *orchards* : enclosures with fruit trees.
3. *fowler* : bird-catcher.
4. *snared* [sneəd] : trapped.
5. *dovecot* : house for doves and pigeons.
6. *cleft* : space between twin trunks of a tree.
7. *pollard elm* : an elm tree which has had the top cut off so that new thin branches will grow.
8. *scurried about* : ran quickly from place to place.
9. *bills* : beaks.
10. *nibbling at* : biting at and eating.
11. *horned cattle* : bulls and cows with horns.
12. *harm* : hurt.
13. *gaunt* : thin and grim.
14. *shutters* : wooden or metal covers for windows.

mule, reading out of a painted book. Sometimes in their green velvet caps, and their jerkins[1] of tanned deerskin,[2] the falconers passed by, with hooded[3] hawks on their wrists. At vintage time[4] came the grape-treaders,[5] with purple hands and feet, wreathed with[6] glossy[7] ivy and carrying dripping skins[8] of wine; and the charcoal-burners sat round their huge braziers[9] at night, watching the dry, logs[10] charring[11] slowly in the fire, and roasting chestnuts in the ashes, and the robbers came out of their caves and made merry with them. Once, too, he had seen a beautiful procession winding up the long dusty road to Toledo. The monks went in front singing sweetly, and carrying bright banners[12] and crosses of gold, and then, in silver armour, with matchlocks[13] and pikes,[14] came the soldiers, and in their midst walked three barefooted men,[15] in strange

1. *jerkins* : a "jerkin" is a type of jacket.
2. *tanned deerskin* : the skin of a deer preserved by tanning, a process used to change raw skin or hide into leather.
3. *hooded* : hoods were placed on the heads of hawks until they were allowed to fly after prey.
4. *vintage time* : the time when grapes are picked for wine.
5. *grape-treaders* : traditionally the juice was pressed out of grapes by treading or standing on them.
6. *wreathed with* : having wreathes of ivy on their heads.
7. *glossy* : shiny.
8. *skins* : bottles made of animal skins.
9. *braziers* : portable stands for holding burning wood or charcoal.
10. *logs* : cut pieces of the branches or trunks of trees.
11. *charring* : burning until they become black.
12. *banners* : flags held on two poles.
13. *matchlocks* : a "matchlock" is a type of gun.
14. *pikes* : weapons with long wooden shaft (handle) and steel head.
15. *three barefooted men* : they would be heretics, on their way to be burned.

yellow dresses painted all over with wonderful figures, and carrying lighted candles in their hands. Certainly there was a great deal to look at in the forest, and when she was tired he would find a soft bank of moss for her, or carry her in his arms, for he was very strong, though he knew that he was not tall. He would make her a necklace of red bryony[1] berries, that would be quite as pretty as the white berries she wore on her dress, and when she was tired of them, she could throw them away, and he would find her others. He would bring her acorn-cups[2] and dew-drenched[3] anemones, and tiny glow-worms[4] to be stars in the pale gold of her hair.

But where was she? He asked the white rose, and it made him no answer. The whole palace seemed asleep, and even where the shutters had not been closed, heavy curtains had been drawn across the windows to keep out the glare. He wandered all round looking for some place through which he might gain an entrance, and at last he caught sight of a little private door that was lying open. He slipped through, and found himself in a splendid hall, far more splendid, he feared, than the forest, there was so much more gilding[5] everywhere, and even the floor was made of great coloured stones, fitted together into a sort of geometrical pattern. But the little Infanta was not there, only some wonderful white statues that

1. *bryony* ['braɪəni] : type of climbing plant with red berries.
2. *acorn-cups* : the cup-like holder of the acorn, the fruit of the oak tree.
3. *dew-drenched* : completely wet with dew.
4. *glow-worms* : beetles whose females emit light.
5. *gilding* : decorations in gold.

looked down on him from their jasper[1] pedestals, with sad blank[2] eyes and strange smiling lips.

At the end of the hall hung a richly embroidered curtain of black velvet, powdered[3] with suns and stars, the King's favourite devices,[4] and broidered[5] on the colour he loved best. Perhaps she was hiding behind that? He would try at any rate.

So he stole[6] quietly across, and drew it aside. No; there was only another room, though a prettier room, he thought, than the one he had just left. The walls were hung with a many-figured green arras[7] of needle-wrought[8] tapestry representing a hunt, the work of some Flemish artists who had spent more than seven years in its composition. It had once been the chamber of *Jean le Fou*, as he was called, that mad King who was so enamoured of the chase,[9] that he had often tried in his delirium to mount[10] the huge rearing[11] horses, and to drag down the stag[12] on which the great hounds were leaping, sounding his hunting horn, and stabbing with his dagger at the pale flying deer. It was now used as the council-room, and on the centre table were lying the red portfolios of the

1. *jasper* : type of quartz.
2. *blank* : expressionless.
3. *powdered* : sprinkled, decorated.
4. *devices* : emblematic designs.
5. *broidered* : sewn.
6. *stole* : moved furtively.
7. *arras* : tapestry, wall-hanging.
8. *needle-wrought* ['ni:dlrɔ:t] : done by needle; embroidered, sewn.
9. *chase* : hunt.
10. *mount* : climb on.
11. *rearing* : of horses - standing up on their hind legs.
12. *stag* : male deer.

ministers, stamped with gold tulips of Spain, and with the arms and emblems of the house of Hapsburg.

The little Dwarf looked in wonder all round him, and was half-afraid to go on. The strange silent horsemen that galloped so swiftly through the long glades [1] without making any noise, seemed to him like those terrible phantoms of whom he had heard the charcoal-burners speaking – the Comprachos, who hunt only at night, and if they meet a man, turn him into a hind,[2] and chase him. But he thought of the pretty Infanta, and took courage. He wanted to find her alone, and tell her that he too loved her. Perhaps she was in the room beyond.

He ran across the soft Moorish carpets, and opened the door. No! She was not here either. The room was quite empty.

It was a throne-room, used for the reception of foreign ambassadors, when the King, which of late had not been often, consented to give them a personal audience; the same room in which, many years before, envoys [3] had appeared from England to make arrangements for the marriage of their Queen, then one of the Catholic sovereigns of Europe, with the Emperor's eldest son. The hangings [4] were of gilt Cordovan leather, and a heavy gilt chandelier with branches for three hundred wax lights hung down from the black and white ceiling. Underneath a great canopy of gold cloth, on which the lions and towers of Castile were broidered in seed pearls, stood the throne itself, covered with a rich pall [5] of black velvet studded with silver tulips and elaborately fringed with silver

1. *glades* : open spaces between trees.
2. *hind* : female deer.
3. *envoys* : messengers, representatives.
4. *hangings* : tapestries.
5. *pall* [pɔːl] : cloth.

and pearls. On the second step of the throne was placed the kneeling-stool[1] of the Infanta, with its cushion of cloth of silver tissue, and below that again, and beyond the limit of the canopy, stood the chair for the Papal Nuncio, who alone had the right to be seated in the King's presence on the occasion of any public ceremonial, and whose Cardinal's hat, with its tangled[2] scarlet tassels,[3] lay on a purple tabouret[4] in front. On the wall facing the throne, hung a life-sized portrait of Charles V in hunting dress, with a great mastiff by his side, and a picture of Philip II receiving the homage of the Netherlands occupied the centre of the other wall. Between the windows stood a black ebony cabinet, inlaid with plates of ivory, on which the figures from Holbein's Dance of Death had been graved[5] – by the hand, some said, of that famous master himself.

But the little Dwarf cared nothing for all this magnificence. He would not have given his rose for all the pearls on the canopy, nor one white petal of his rose for the throne itself. What he wanted was to see the Infanta before she went down to the pavilion, and to ask her to come away with him when he had finished his dance. Here, in the Palace, the air was close and heavy, but in the forest the wind blew free, and the sunlight with wandering hands of gold moved the tremulous leaves aside. There were flowers, too, in the forest, not so splendid, perhaps, as the flowers in the garden, but more sweetly scented[6] for all that;

1. *kneeling-stool* : stool on which the Infanta knelt before the King on ceremonial occasions.
2. *tangled* : intertwined; in a confused mass.
3. *tassels* : bunches of threads tied at one end.
4. *tabouret* ['tæbərɪt] : stool.
5. *graved* : engraved.
6. *scented* : perfumed.

hyacinths in early spring that flooded[1] with waving[2] purple the cool glens,[3] and grassy knolls;[4] yellow primroses that nestled[5] in little clumps[6] round the gnarled[7] roots of the oak-trees; bright celandine, and blue speedwell, and irises lilac and gold. There were grey catkins on the hazels, and the foxgloves drooped with the weight of their dappled[8] bee-haunted[9] cells. The chestnut had its spires[10] of white stars, and the hawthorn its pallid moons of beauty. Yes: surely she would come if he could only find her! She would come with him to the fair forest, and all day long he would dance for her delight. A smile lit up his eyes at the thought, and he passed into the next room.

Of all the rooms this was the brightest and the most beautiful. The walls were covered with pink-flowered Lucca damask,[11] patterned with birds and dotted[12] with dainty[13] blossoms of silver, the furniture was of massive silver, festooned with[14] florid wreaths, and swinging[15] Cupids; in front of the two large fire-places stood great screens broidered with

1. *flooded* : covered completely.
2. *waving* : moving in the wind.
3. *glens* : valleys.
4. *knolls* : small round hills.
5. *nestled* : settled comfortably.
6. *clumps* : groups, (especially of trees and plants).
7. *gnarled* [na:ld] : twisted and covered with protuberances.
8. *dappled* : variegated, with patches of different colours.
9. *bee-haunted* : frequented by bees.
10. *spires* : tall cone-shaped structures.
11. *damask* : woven material with a pattern.
12. *dotted* : marked at intervals.
13. *dainty* : delicate.
14. *festooned* [fe'stu:nd] *with* : hung with chains of.
15. *swinging* : hanging and free to move in different directions.

parrots and peacocks, and the floor, which was of sea-green onyx,[1] seemed to stretch far away into the distance. Nor was he alone. Standing under the shadow of the doorway, at the extreme end of the room, he saw a little figure watching him. His heart trembled, a cry of joy broke from his lips, and he moved out into the sunlight. As he did so, the figure moved out also, and he saw it plainly.

The Infanta! It was a monster, the most grotesque monster he had ever beheld. Not properly shaped as all other people were, but hunchbacked,[2] and crooked-limbed,[3] with a huge lolling[4] head and mane of black hair. The little Dwarf frowned, and the monster frowned also. He laughed, and it laughed with him, and held its hands to its sides, just as he himself was doing. He made it a mocking bow, and it returned him a low reverence. He went towards it, and it came to meet him, copying each step that he made, and stopping when he stopped himself. He shouted with amusement, and ran forward, and reached out his hand, and the hand of the monster touched his, and it was as cold as ice. He grew afraid, and moved his hand across, and the monster's hand followed it quickly. He tried to press on,[5] but something smooth and hard stopped him. The face of the monster was now close to his own, and seemed full of terror. He brushed his hair off his eyes. It imitated him. He struck at it, and it returned blow for blow.[6] He loathed[7] it, and

1. *onyx* ['ɒnɪks] : a kind of stone with different colours in layers.
2. *hunchbacked* : with a hunch or hump on his back.
3. *crooked-limbed* [krʊkɪd'lɪmd] : with limbs that are not straight.
4. *lolling* : hanging.
5. *press on* : continue on his way.
6. *blow for blow* : as the dwarf struck at the figure in the mirror each of his blows seemed to be returned.
7. *loathed* : hated and felt contempt for.

it made hideous faces at him. He drew back, and it retreated.

What was it? He thought for a moment, and looked round at the rest of the room. It was strange, but everything seemed to have its double in this invisible wall of clear water. Yes, picture for picture was repeated, and couch for couch. The sleeping Faun that lay in the alcove by the doorway had its twin brother that slumbered,[1] and the silver Venus that stood in the sunlight held out her arms to a Venus as lovely as herself.

Was it Echo? He had called to her once in the valley, and she had answered him word for word. Could she mock the eye, as she mocked the voice? Could she make a mimic world just like the real world? Could the shadows of things have colours and life and movement? Could it be that – ?

He started, and taking from his breast the beautiful white rose, he turned round, and kissed it. The monster had a rose of its own, petal for petal the same! It kissed it with like kisses, and pressed it to his heart with horrible gestures.

When the truth dawned on him, he gave a wild cry of despair, and fell sobbing[2] to the ground. So it was he who was misshapen and hunchbacked, foul[3] to look at and grotesque. He himself was the monster, and it was at him that all the children had been laughing, and the little Princess who he had thought loved him – she, too, had been merely mocking at his ugliness, and making merry over his twisted limbs. Why had they not left him in the forest, where there was no mirror to tell him how loathsome[4] he was? Why had

1. *slumbered* : slept.
2. *sobbing* : weeping uncontrollably.
3. *foul* : ugly.
4. *loathsome* : repulsive, causing disgust.

his father not killed him, rather than sell him to his shame? The hot tears poured down his cheeks, and he tore the white rose to pieces. The sprawling[1] monster did the same, and scattered the faint petals in the air. It grovelled[2] on the ground, and, when he looked at it, it watched him with a face drawn[3] with pain. He crept away, lest he should see it, and covered his eyes with his hands. He crawled, like some wounded thing, into the shadow, and lay there moaning.[4]

And at that moment the Infanta herself came in with her companions through the open window, and when they saw the ugly little dwarf lying on the ground and beating the floor with his clenched hands, in the most fantastic and exaggerated manner, they went off into shouts of happy laughter, and stood all round him and watched him.

'His dancing was funny,' said the Infanta; 'but his acting is funnier still. Indeed, he is almost as good as the puppets, only, of course, not quite so natural.' And she fluttered her big fan and applauded.

But the little Dwarf never looked up, and his sobs grew fainter and fainter, and suddenly he gave a curious gasp,[5] and clutched his side. And then he fell back again, and lay quite still.

'That is capital,' said the Infanta, after a pause; 'but now you must dance for me.'

'Yes,' cried the children, 'you must get up and dance, for you are as clever as the Barbary apes, and much more ridiculous.'

But the little Dwarf made no answer.

1. *sprawling* : lying shapelessly on the floor.
2. *grovelled* : lay in complete humiliation.
3. *drawn* : distorted.
4. *moaning* : making sounds that expressed his suffering.
5. *gasp* : convulsive catching of his breath.

And the Infanta stamped[1] her foot, and called out to her uncle, who was walking on the terrace with the Chamberlain, reading some dispatches[2] that had just arrived from Mexico, where the Holy Office had recently been established. 'My funny little dwarf is sulking,'[3] she cried, 'you must wake him up and tell him to dance for me.'

They smiled at each other, and sauntered in,[4] and Don Pedro stooped[5] down, and slapped[6] the Dwarf on the cheek with his embroidered glove, 'You must dance,' he said, '*petit monstre*. You must dance. The Infanta of Spain and the Indies wishes to be amused.'

But the little Dwarf never moved.

'A whipping master[7] should be sent for,' said Don Pedro wearily,[8] and he went back to the terrace. But the Chamberlain looked grave, and he knelt beside the little Dwarf, and put his hand upon his heart. And after a few moments he shrugged his shoulders, and rose up, and having made a low bow to the Infanta he said –

'*Mi bella Princesa*, your funny little dwarf will never dance again. It is a pity, for he is so ugly that he might have made the King smile.'

'But why will he not dance again?' asked the Infanta, laughing.

1. *stamped* : brought her foot down heavily on the floor, as a sign of anger and impatience.
2. *dispatches* : messages, official communications.
3. *sulking* : behaving in an unsociable, bad-tempered way.
4. *sauntered in* : walked in unhurriedly.
5. *stooped* : bent.
6. *slapped* : hit sharply with the flat of the hand.
7. *whipping master* : an official of the court who whipped offenders.
8. *wearily* : tiredly, languidly.

'Because his heart is broken,' answered the Chamberlain.

And the Infanta frowned, and her dainty rose-leaf lips curled [1] in pretty disdain. [2] 'For the future let those who come to play with me have no hearts,' she cried, and she ran out into the garden.

1. *curled* : moved up (usually refers to the top lip); sneered.
2. *disdain* : scorn, contempt.

Pre-reading Activity

Look at reproductions of paintings by Velasquez (1599-1660), who, as court painter to Philip IV of Spain in Madrid, painted the two Spanish infantas of the 1650s, especially the Infanta Margarita. In "Las Meninas" ("The Maids of Honour"), with Margarita we can also see two of the court dwarfs. "Wilde's description of the princess, king, and dwarf all seem inspired by the paintings, ritual, and sombre splendour of the Spanish court of that time." (Isobel Murray: *Oscar Wilde: Complete Shorter Fiction,* Oxford World's Classics, p. 269.)

Activities while Reading

The story is divided into four sections:

Section 1 (pp. 165-71);

Section 2 (pp. 171-80);

Section 3 (pp. 180-8);

Section 4 (pp. 188-98).

Section 1 (pp. 165-71)

1. After saying how important the people of the country felt it was for the Infanta to have a fine day for her birthday, Wilde goes on to describe the day in terms of the reactions to "the wonderful sunlight" of the tulips, the butterflies, the lizards, the pomegranates, the lemons and the magnolia trees. How do each of these react to the sunlight?

Plants and Creatures	Reaction to the Sunlight
tulips	
butterflies	
lizards	
pomegranates	
lemons	
magnolia trees	

2. List the colours that Wilde refers to.

3. How are the trellis and arcades transformed by the sunlight?

4. What sense apart from sight is appealed to in the description of the day?

5. What is the overall impression created by this opening description?

6. In the next paragraph Wilde describes the Infanta and her companions.

- **a.** What is unusual about her companions today, on her birthday?
- **b.** What is the quality that Wilde notes about the way these slim Spanish children move?
- **c.** In what way is the Infanta superior to the other children?
- **d.** What impression does Wilde create in the description of the Infanta's clothes?

7. In the next paragraph ("From a window in the palace...") Wilde introduces the King, the Infanta's father. He makes a great contrast between the King's sadness and his daughter's vivacity.
   a. What words in this paragraph convey the King's state of mind?
   b. What words associated with death are used to describe the King's dead wife?

8. In what way is Wilde ironical about the celebration of the wedding of the King and his young wife?

9. What criticism did many people make of the King's behaviour towards his young wife?

10. What was the King's reaction to the death of his wife?

11. The Infanta, on the day of her birthday, reminded the King of his wife. What qualities and behaviour does the Infanta share with her mother, who died so young?

12. Describe the Infanta's feelings when her father disappears.

SECTION 2 (pp. 171-80)

Read the first two paragraphs of this section.

1. Guess the meanings of the following words, then check them in your monolingual dictionary.

WORD	YOUR GUESS	DICTIONARY DEFINITION
flitted		
hind legs		
dismounted		
plunged		
disclosed		

2. In the parade of "toreadors" and the "bull-fight", what words suggest the following?

BRIGHTNESS AND COLOUR	
MOVEMENT	
COMEDY	

3. After the bull-fight come the Italian puppets, the African juggler, the solemn minuet, the troop of handsome "Egyptians", with their bear and Barbary apes. Pick out words and phrases which describe and bring to life the nature of the entertainment each provides.

ITALIAN PUPPETS	
AFRICAN JUGGLER	
SOLEMN MINUET	
'EGYPTIANS'	
BEAR	
BARBARY APES	

4. The climax of the morning's entertainment was the Dwarf's dancing.
a. What words convey the grotesqueness of the Dwarf?
b. What contrast is there between the Dwarf and the Princess and her companions?

5. For what does Wilde criticise the Spanish court in the passage describing the Dwarf?

6. What was perhaps the most amusing thing about the Dwarf?
7. How does the Princess respond to the Dwarf's performance and what does the Dwarf feel about the Princess?

SECTION 3 (pp. 180-8)

1. How does the Dwarf react to the news that he is to dance again before the Infanta, at her own request?
2. What reactions does the Dwarf cause when he enters the Royal Garden?

	REACTIONS
FLOWERS	
CACTUS	
WHITE ROSE-TREE	
SUNDIAL	
PEACOCK	
BIRDS	
LIZARDS	

3. Why did the birds and the lizards like the Dwarf?
4. What did the Dwarf feel about everything in the garden?
5. Why were the Flowers "excessively annoyed" at the behaviour of the birds and the lizards. In what way are the flowers like the people of the court?
6. The last long paragraph of the section describes the life in the forest that the Dwarf believes he could share with the Princess, who, he thinks, has fallen in love with him. It describes what the Dwarf knows of forest life and the things he will do for the Infanta. List three things that the Dwarf knows and three things he would do for the Princess.

THINGS THE DWARF KNOWS	THINGS THE DWARF WOULD DO FOR THE INFANTA

7. Name the people that the Dwarf sees in the forest.

SECTION 4 (pp. 188-98)

1. What details does the Dwarf notice in each of the first three rooms he enters?

THE SPLENDID HALL	
THE COUNCIL-ROOM	
THE THRONE-ROOM	

2. Why does Wilde include such detailed description of all this splendour?

3. What is the Dwarf's reaction to all the magnificence he sees around him?

4. What contrast does the Dwarf make between the Palace and the forest?

5. When the Dwarf sees a little figure at the extreme end of the fourth room, at first who does he think it is?

6. Describe the reactions of the Dwarf to his reflection.
7. How does the Dwarf come to realize he is looking at his own reflection? What is his reaction when he realizes the truth?
8. Describe the behaviour of the Infanta and her companions when they find the Dwarf lying on the ground beating the floor with his clenched hands.
9. Comment on the Infanta's response to the death of the Dwarf.

Post-reading Activities

Wilde's Language and Style

Description

1. Which of the following descriptions would you think suitable to the way the tale is told?

fast-moving	highly visual	gentle and sensitive
at times ironic	told from one point of view	with a great deal of authorial intrusion into the narrative

Give reasons for your answers.

2. In this story, Wilde's language is very often descriptive. (You have already answered some questions on his descriptions.) Now list the different categories of description in the story, e.g. dress (particularly the way the Infanta is dressed for her birthday).

3. Let us look more closely at two descriptions:
   a. of the tapestry in the council-room, which represents a hunt. How does Wilde suggest the sense of movement in the picture?
   b. of the throne-room.
      i) How does Wilde suggest the richness and splendour of this chamber?
      ii) How does he suggest a more sinister atmosphere in the room?

Characterisation

1. Write character-sketches of the two principal characters, the Infanta and the Dwarf.
2. Write notes on the characterisation of the King and of his brother, Don Pedro.

Narrative Technique

1. The story is in four sections. Give a title to each.
2. The story is not told chronologically, that is in the order in which all the events mentioned took place. Which parts of the story do not take place on the Infanta's birthday?
3. From what different points of view do we observe what happens in the story?

The Presence of Wilde in the Story

1. Wilde's presence in the text is most evident in his comments on the court. Go carefully through the text and note these comments. What impression does he give us of the Spanish court?
2. Wilde always shows a sympathy for the "outsider", someone rejected by society (there are, no doubt, biographical reasons for this). Note any points in the presentaton of the Dwarf which indicate Wilde's sympathy for him.

Themes

Important themes in the story are:

- the contrast between Art and Nature;
- the association of beauty with cruelty;
- the contrast between outer ugliness and inner beauty;
- the contrast between the simple life of the forest and the splendour and sophistication of the court;
- the outsider, the figure rejected by society;
- the physically abnormal regarded as a figure to be derided rather than one requiring acceptance and sympathetic understanding.

Make comments on these themes, trying to rank them in order of importance, giving reasons for your conclusions.

Summarising

Complete the following summary of the story by filling the gaps. The infinitives of verbs required are given in brackets.

It ....(be) the day of the birthday of the Infanta of Spain. Seeing the young Princess's happiness, the King ....(remind) of his wife, who ....(die) young. In his .... he .... (retire) to the chapel where his dead wife ....(lie). Meanwhile the Princess and her friends .... (entertain). First came the ...., followed by Italian puppets and then an African .... After a solemn .... and the entertainment .... (provide) by a group of gipsies came the .... part of the the entertainment, a grotesque dance by a dwarf. The most amusing thing about the dwarf was his complete lack of .... of how .... he was. In fact, when the Princess laughed at his performance and at the end .... (throw) him a white rose, he felt she ....(fall) in love with him. When he heard that she wanted him to dance for her again, he ran out into the garden in a state of .... Unable to find the Princess anywhere he ....(imagine) what life ....(be) like with her if she joined him in the forest, his home. Entering the palace in search of her, he ....(wander) through the rooms until he came to a room with a large mirror in which he saw his .... When he .... (realize) the image in the mirror was of himself, he .... (horrify) and threw himself to the floor, ...(moan). At this point the Infanta and her friends entered the room. Seeing the dwarf lying on the ground beating the floor with his .... fists, the children .... (laugh) and the Princess, ...(say) his .... was even funnier than his ...., applauded. But the little Dwarf never looked up. When the Chamberlain explained that the Dwarf .... (die) of a .... heart, the Infanta only frowned and said that anyone who came to play with her in future ....(have) no heart.

Notes

Notes

Notes

Notes

Notes

Notes

Notes

Notes

Notes

Notes

Notes

Notes